# Great Chefs Cook
# Vegan

# Great Chefs Cook

# *Vegan*

## Linda Long

**GIBBS SMITH**
TO ENRICH AND INSPIRE HUMANKIND

Salt Lake City | Charleston | Santa Fe | Santa Barbara

*To Walter Feldesman, for your friendship and heartfelt encouragement during the creation of this book—from witnessing my "lightbulb" moment of inspiration, to treating me to so many vegan dinners of the great chefs, but mostly for the wonderful conversations that happened during them. I am deeply, deeply grateful.*

*And to Gladys and Floyd, my late parents, proud proprietors of the Dixie Truck Stop & Diner along old Pennsylvania Route 11, who instilled the exhilaration of sharing good food with others.*

First Edition
12 11 10 09 08    5 4 3 2 1

Text and photographs © 2008 Linda Long

Published by
Gibbs Smith
P.O. Box 667
Layton, Utah 84041

1-800.835.4993 orders
www.gibbs-smith.com

Designed and produced by Howard Klein
Printed and bound in Hong Kong

Library of Congress Cataloging-in-Publication Data

Long, Linda, 1942–
  Great chefs cook vegan / Linda Long. — 1st ed.
      p. cm.
  Includes index.
  ISBN-13: 978-1-4236-0153-1
  ISBN-10: 1-4236-0153-X
  1.  Vegan cookery. 2.  Cooks—United States.  I. Title.
  TX837.L625 2008
  641.5'636—dc22

                    2008007977

# Contents

# Acknowledgments

My first cookbook! But I feel too guilty just saying "my" as it is not the truth. It is a compilation of so many people. The stars are the chefs and their amazing and devoted support teams of chef de cuisines, sous chefs, and assistants. Their embracing of the vision for this book is astounding. It is impossible to adequately thank them. It is also staggering to discover how many old and new friends came together to create this book. It reminds me of the scrolling credits at the end of a film. Most people pay little attention to them yet they all gave something of themselves to see the project come into existence. I honor all who gave something of themselves for this book as they have honored me with their dedication. It warms my heart with unspeakable gratitude and moist eyes.

To deal with the fears and endless questions of a first-time author, and to keep me on a timeline (not easy with a Sagittarian), I acknowledge my editor, **Melissa Barlow,** at Gibbs Smith. Her patience with my lamenting dissertations and her ability to turn me around with a fast one-sentence positive outlook is something to behold.

Thanks to **Sharon Van Vechten,** for sharing vast knowledge and relationships with the people at the top of the culinary world. Daily e-mails for nearly two years were relentlessly encouraging, and for even daring the tasks of a photographer's assistant for a couple food shoots! Her top-notch marketing and promotional talents will extend beyond this writing. There is none better.

There would not be a glossary if not for **Jane Belt,** home economist and vegan friend who helped to identify and define terms from the chef's recipes and define them. And test beet recipes—her least favorite food! Her work ethic was contagious and we always agreed upon when to take breaks for chocolate or beautiful lunches on nice trays with linen napkins and flowers. We cannot help our home ec roots!

Beginning with the book proposal and then with final pages, I appreciate dear longtime friends **Dotti Kauffman,** author, and **Linda Lombri,** editor, both so busy with their own lives, for taking time to look over my submissions so I did not embarrass myself too much. I thank accomplished writer **Sarah Lewis,** for her friendship and expert suggestions along the way.

**Joanne Black, Francine Epstein, Dusty Stamper,** and **Josephine Hall** have the ability to hone into the bottom line of any situation. I thank them for knowing me so well and setting me straight at strategic moments.

It took love of food to test and make good notes. Joining me in testing and rewriting recipes were brilliant home economist friends **Connie Binns, Jane Belt, Ronda Martinez, Sarah Ott** (who also involved husband **Henry**), **Judy Lindahl,** and **Cathy DeVries.** Since the chefs were located around the country, some also provided housing, and transportation, and served as photo assistants—beyond the call of duty.

Some recipes required a professional tester, and **Carliss Pond** soldiered forward in that capacity time after time. **Melissa Maly** tackled and won when testing the raw vegan offerings. I am very grateful.

The students at Secchia Institute for Culinary Education at Grand Rapids Community College were enthusiastic to learn while testing some of the food of the great chefs they had only heard about in the media. Huge thanks to **Professor Kevin Dunn** and his select students who assisted, among them was the now-graduated and talented **Joel Boone.** I owe special thanks to now-graduated **Joshua Siudyla,** who tested frequently, sometimes retesting problem recipes, eager to find clearer procedures. I am watching the star futures of these talented chefs-in-the-making. I will always remember them.

Sometimes, I asked vegan chefs to come to my rescue. Thanks to exciting **Chef Cathi DiCocoa,** masterful **Chef Saulau Tupolo,** super creative visionary **Chef Tal Ronnen,**

6

and tireless caterer **Chef Del Sroufe** and international entrepreneur **Chef Chad Sarno.**

Some vegan chefs are friends who have their own cookbooks and understood the need to assist me through the process, such as dear friend, the extraordinary **Fran Costigan** (*More Great Good Dairy-Free Desserts*), whose lusty chocolate cake must be the main event at my birthday each year! Thanks to forever energetic **Chef Beverly Lynn Bennent** (*Complete Idiot's Guide to Vegan Living*), **Jill Nussinow** (*The Veggie Queen*) and multi-cookbook author **Bryanna Clark Grogan** (*Nonna's Italian Kitchen*).

American Vegan Society president **Freya Dinshah,** and cookbook author (*The Vegan Kitchen*) tested and gave me support in so many ways. North Carolina's Triangle Vegetarian Society president **Dilip Barman** not only tested but offered advance publicity on their popular website. **Bob "Vegan Bob" Irish,** supporter of vegan causes, gave constant encouragement.

A few New York–based students and interns require special accolades when it came to testing, rewriting the tested recipes and incorporating the tester's notes; I was truly blessed to have found **Victoria Fernandez, Berthsy Ayide,** and **Hannah Hoffman. Amy Mekemson** was there to add her help when it really counted. Thanks to the staff at New York University's Elmer Holmes Bobst Library for some of the great interns.

And sometimes I turned to really good home cooks. Thanks to my sister, **Aileen Sharar,** and hometown friends **Bobbi Boock,** and her restaurateur husband, **Tom Boock.** Thanks to **Chef Neil Annis** for standing by to solve any culinary questions.

Besides recipes to test there were many photos to take of the wonderful food. Those who were especially interested in photography and worked tirelessly were **Anita Lombri, Helene Seligman,** and **Sarah Jonard.** Photographer **Mellissa Mallow** was endlessly helpful not only in correcting some of my photos but in patiently teaching me some valuable techniques over the phone!

Special thanks to **Sandee Garihan, Inger Lonmo,** and **Diane Fleck** for being willing to assist with a restaurant shoot. It would have been difficult without you.

When it comes to retouching photos there is nobody better than photographer Dan Demetriad who saved me in the last moments, and **Maria Ferrari** who helped me along the way and who deserves every accolade for her fine work as a teacher and photographer. Interns **Jarrett Baston** often came to my aid as did **Kelly Murdoch-Kitt.** Oh my! Thank you!

**Amie Hamlin** and **Nathalie Stewart** gladly shared their inside information for contacts. **Mary Anne Symons Brown** shared her exciting marketing talents.

And, thanks to **Lou Manna,** food photographer, for allowing me to practice at his studio. Thanks to **Keith Johnson** at B&H for setting me on the right path with the perfectly chosen equipment and for being patient with my dense questions and endless e-mails, to **Ron Herald** at Calumet for being willing to field my emergency calls from the road about equipment settings, and to the men at The Lens & Repro Equipment for their emergency repairs and guidance.

A thanks forward to my dear friend Paula Al-Sabah, who promised to buy many copies, even in Kuwait!

Finally, there are two men who truly made this book possible. **Walter Feldesman** (a most amazing man) took me to many of the restaurants to sample the food and meet the chefs, a cost that would have been out of range otherwise. His enchantment in imagining this book kept me enthused. Had I not met the incredible and very tall **Gibbs Smith,** quite by chance, at a book trade show and mentioned my idea to his immediate enthusiasm, who knows where this idea might be right now. A forever thank you to both of them far beyond these words!

# Introduction

After growing up in the restaurant business, being vegan for several decades and living in New York City where the restaurants are among the best in the world, I have had my share of experiences trying to order plant-based food from menus. To the surprise of many chefs, no vegetarians want to be offered a plate of unseasoned and overcooked vegetables. And, we don't want to be stuck with a plate of pasta every time we go out to eat with our friends.

There are some really wonderful vegan restaurants and I have found all my friends truly enjoy them with me from time to time. However, people go out to share a meal and talk, and it is fun to try all kinds of restaurants.

Launching the idea to write a cookbook happened unexpectedly. Because of a wonderful gentleman, Walter Feldesman, who loves eating at the top restaurants, I had the opportunity to dine at two of the best, Jean-Georges and davidburke & donatella. When making the reservation at Jean-Georges, I mentioned that there would be one vegan and would that be a problem? I was told that it would not be. Once seated in the beautiful windowed space overlooking a winter snow scene at Columbus Circle, I was handed a menu. I told the waiter that I was the vegan on the reservation and perhaps would not need the menu. He left for the kitchen and came back to say, "The chef has planned black truffle dumplings with pumpkin puree and tiny diced cubes of celery and yellow zucchini topped with maple sake foam." Not even a mention of a plate of vegetables! I talked about that dining experience for a long time afterward.

A few weeks later at davidburke & donatella, David came out to the table himself to ask a few questions. He would not tell me what he was going to serve but an amusing smile emerged as he went to the kitchen. Soon, I was served what he called a Vegetable Torte. I called it a Vegetable "Carousel." It was a perfectly molded circle piled high with colorful and beautifully prepared and seasoned vegetables, topped with mashed potatoes that had been leveled flat to hold a border of perfectly spaced peas around the top edge. After the joy of eating this creation, we discussed the protein content, and David suggested that adding any kind of beans as one of the layers would work well. Clearly, this was a dish that could be adapted endlessly.

I wanted to really experiment now. I encouraged Walter to consider reserving at other top restaurants and see how more great chefs did things. He was game, and eventually he began tasting my food and wanted to order as I did, stating that he could not believe he was eating so much plant food and loving it. So, on to Chef Gabriel Kreuther, then at the Ritz-Carlton on Central Park South, now at The Modern at The Museum of Modern Art. When the amuse-bouche (the tiny one-bite starter) came, I remembered that I had forgotten to state at reservation that a vegan meal was needed. I was upset as I know how a busy kitchen can be disrupted with a last-minute request. However, the waiter put me at ease and when the first course arrived I was given a dish that I will remember forever. It was a beautifully plated piece of grilled watermelon cut into a perfect inch-high flat circle with the entire round edge covered with overlapping soft sun-dried tomatoes, just high enough to create a lip at the top edge to hold a layer of roasted pistachios covering the top, all placed on top of lines of reduced sweet balsamic vinegar.

New Year's Eve can be a problem but Chef Daniel Boulud made it happen at Daniel, always listed with the top restaurants in the country. Walter and I were joined by vegan friend Inger Lonmo, who has been on a lot of this journey with me. We enjoyed the "gazillion-dollar" tasting menu created just for the occasion. The feast began with an astounding small box with a lid made of potatoes packed full of grains and black and white truffles, and ended with a huge box made of dark chocolate filled with many chocolate morsels. It was great to see that this time I did not have to remind the chef that chocolate is a plant!

I told Walter that I think there were too many people who had no idea that these chefs were making this level of creative vegan food. As a home economist with deep roots in food, it occurred to me that perhaps I should combine my love of food and photography to share my exciting discoveries. It was all getting too good to keep as a secret. I should write a book!

I approached the chefs who first impressed me and was thrilled when the first one said, "I'll be in it!" As I asked others, they often commented that they get bored preparing animal products over and over as there are only so many ways to work with them; but plant foods—vegetables, fruits, grains,

beans, nuts, and seeds—provide endless options for fabulous dishes, as was evident to see when these great chefs prepared dishes that are included in this book in their own restaurant kitchens and were photographed in their dining rooms.

Each chef was asked to offer a vegan menu of three to four courses. The great Chef Charlie Trotter of Charlie Trotter's in Chicago had his top chef, Chef Matthias Merges, prepare an entire tasting menu. Often several recipes are needed to make one special dish. It is exciting to realize that many of these recipes can be lifted out to become its own dish, such as making a sorbet and eating it alone, or making a sauce that can be used in your own way.

I learned a lot about plating. Since there were no food stylists (as chefs will not allow anyone to touch their food) I watched as they created their plates. It occurred to me that all the components end up on the plate. Where they land can be a wonderful creative experience, and it adds an exciting dimension to serving and sharing any food.

Most chefs like to have a three-day notice to prepare your fabulous vegan experience in their restaurants as I learned from noticing that the incomparable Chef Thomas Keller, upon opening Per Se, had a nine-course vegetarian tasting menu. I told him that I wanted to come but that the offerings were heavily dairy-laden. He was quick to solve that by saying, "We can make it vegan. Just give us about three days." And, so I did and so did he. Wow!

If you cannot get to the thirteen cities and twenty-five chefs in this book, just turn the page and take a bite!

# Alex Stratta

*"When the heart and essence of culinary arts are applied to vegan cuisine, it exemplifies the importance of top-quality ingredients and time-tested techniques to create flavorful and extraordinary new dishes."*

Alessandro "Alex" Stratta's refined cuisine marries the finest and freshest French Riviera and Italian ingredients. Coming from a long line of restaurateurs and hoteliers, Stratta found his culinary calling early in life, working in some of the world's finest hotel kitchens. One of his mentors, Alain Ducasse, introduced him to the highest level of passion, dedication, and discipline for his craft at Louis XV at the Hotel de Paris in Monaco. Daniel Boulud at Le Cirque in New York further elevated his natural culinary talents and management and organizational skills.

At twenty-four, Stratta was named executive chef of Mary Elaine's at the world-class Phoenician in Phoenix. The restaurant became a premier dining destination and established Stratta's national reputation. Leading hotelier Steve Wynn selected Stratta to head the Renoir at the Mirage Hotel and Casino in Las Vegas, and he subsequently opened his namesake restaurant Alex at the Las Vegas Wynn. His sophisticated vegetarian tasting menus and his other signature dishes have garnered Mobil Five-Star, AAA Five-Diamond, and top Zagat ratings. In addition, he has won James Beard Foundation awards as a top dining destination, America's top hotel chef, and Best Chef: Southwest.

# Chilled Provençal Vegetables in Jicama "Cannelloni" with Red Pepper Jus and Artichoke Sauté

SERVES 8

### RED PEPPER JUS

5 red bell peppers
1 tablespoon extra virgin olive oil
Salt and pepper to taste

### CANDIED ORANGE ZEST

2 cups fresh orange zest
1 cup granulated sugar
2 cups fresh lemon juice
½ teaspoon aged sherry vinegar
Salt to taste

To make the Red Pepper Jus: Cut the peppers in half and remove the seeds. Juice the peppers in a vegetable juicer, or if unavailable, cut into quarters and add to a food processor or high-speed blender with a small amount of water added slowly until a "tomato juice" consistency, and then strain. Heat bell pepper juice in a saucepan over medium heat until reduced to ¼ cup and then pour into a blender. Mix on low, slowly adding the oil until smooth. Season with salt and pepper, and chill until needed.

To make the Candied Orange Zest: Place orange zest in a shallow bowl of cold water. Blanch the zest three times, moving from cold water to boiling water and straining in between. In a saucepan, dissolve sugar in the lemon juice and bring to a simmer. Add blanched zest and simmer over low heat until zest is soft but not caramelized; remove from heat. Add vinegar and season with salt. Reserve zest in syrup for up to 1 week in the refrigerator.

## SEASONED OLIVE OIL

½ cup extra virgin olive oil

2 sprigs thyme

3 teaspoons raw garlic purée
(store-bought tubes)

## STUFFING

1 cup finely diced white onion

1 cup finely diced red bell pepper

1 cup finely diced eggplant

1 cup finely diced zucchini

2 tablespoons dried currants, soaked
in sherry vinegar until bloomed

2 tablespoons roughly chopped
toasted pine nuts

2 tablespoons Candied Orange Zest
(recipe on facing page)

1 tablespoon chopped black olives

2 tablespoons diced tomato confit

1 tablespoon chopped basil

Salt and pepper to taste

1 tablespoon Per Me olive oil (or
high-quality extra virgin olive oil)

## "CANNELLONI"

1 to 2 large jicama bulbs

2 cups Stuffing (recipe above)

## ARTICHOKES

2 medium artichokes

1 tablespoon olive oil

2 cloves garlic

1 teaspoon fresh thyme leaves

Salt and pepper to taste

## GARNISH

1 bunch purple basil, tops only

4 radishes, thinly sliced

1 bunch chives, minced

Sprigs of flat-leaf parsley

Fleur de sel to taste

To make the Seasoned Olive Oil: Combine the oil, thyme, and garlic in a saucepan and heat until well blended, assuring that the "raw garlic" flavor is gone.

To make the Stuffing: Cook the onion, bell pepper, eggplant, and zucchini separately in 2 tablespoons each of the hot Seasoned Olive Oil. Drain separately on paper towels. Combine currants, pine nuts, Candied Orange Zest, olives, tomato confit, basil, salt, and pepper. Add drained vegetables and combine with the Per Me olive oil until it holds the consistency of paste.

To make the "Cannelloni": Peel the jicama and, using a mandolin, cut 24 paper-thin slices that are 3½ x 3 inches. Place slices lengthwise on a clean surface. Using a teaspoon, place a line of Stuffing across the bottom one-fourth of the square. Gently roll around the filling, tucking in the end and rolling into a tight cylinder (about ⅛ inch thick). If filling has fallen out of the rolls, restuff using the flat side of a small rubber spatula; this will give them a clean, consistent look. Refrigerate for 2 hours, or until needed.

To make the Artichokes: To attain the artichoke hearts, cut off the stems of the artichokes with scissors or a small sharp knife, remove and discard the choke, and then trim where necessary. Heat a heavy saucepan over medium heat with the oil. Add whole artichoke hearts and cook to a sweat. Add garlic and thyme. Season lightly with salt and pepper. Cover with water and bring to a rapid boil. Reduce heat and simmer until tender. Chill and reserve until needed.

How to Plate: Slice artichoke hearts into ⅛-inch-thick slices and fan in the center of an oval plate. Spoon 1 to 2 teaspoons of Red Pepper Jus around the slices. Arrange three of the "Cannelloni" on top of artichokes. Finish with a few leaves of basil, radish slices, chives, parsley, and a sprinkle of fleur de sel. Serve chilled.

# *Roasted Beet Salad with Pistachios and Aged Balsamic Vinegar*

8 SERVINGS

### BABY BEETS

8 baby Chioggia beets

8 baby yellow beets

8 baby red beets

### BEET CHIPS

1 large red beet

1 large yellow beet

1 cup simple syrup (1 to 1 ratio sugar
    and hot water, until sugar dissolves)

### ROASTED BEETS

4 large red beets

4 large yellow beets

¼ cup water

6 sprigs thyme

Salt to taste

**To make the Baby Beets:** Rinse and trim the beets. Blanch them separately (to prevent color bleeding) for approximately 5 minutes in salted boiling water. Remove beets and place in ice water until cool enough to touch, and then rub off the skins using a damp kitchen towel. Keeping colors separate, cut beets in half or in quarters (depending on the size). Refrigerate until needed for up to 2 days.

**To make the Beet Chips:** Using a mandolin or very sharp knife, slice beets into paper thin slices and cut into uniform circles with a 2-inch-round cutter. Divide warm simple syrup into two bowls. Place beet slices in bowls by color. Remove beets from the syrup, brushing off any excess, and place in a single layer on a flat baking sheet fitted with a Silpat; place a second Silpat on top. Bake in a preheated 300-degree F, low-fan convection oven for 10 minutes, or a 325-degree F conventional oven. Rotate pan and bake 5 minutes more. Rotate again and bake for another 5 minutes to complete a total baking time of 20 minutes, or until crisp. Cool the beets and store in a covered container at room temperature for up to 2 days.

**To make the Roasted Beets:** Preheat a low-fan convection oven to 325 degrees F, or in a conventional oven to 350 degrees F. Rinse beets well and place in a deep heavy pan with water, thyme, and salt. Cover tightly with foil and roast for 2 to 3 hours, or until thoroughly cooked and tender. Check water throughout roasting process. If water evaporates before beets are tender, add just enough water to steam the beets; remove from oven. Once cooled, cut beets into ½-inch-thick slices. Cut slices with a 1-inch-round fluted cookie cutter, keeping the colors separate.

## SHAVED BEETS

2 baby Chioggia beets
2 baby yellow beets
2 baby red beets
1 tablespoon olive oil
2 teaspoons minced chives
Salt and pepper to taste

## SALAD

4 heads Tom Thumb or other mild
  baby lettuce
24 leaves red ribbon sorrel

## VINAIGRETTE

Salt and pepper to taste
1 part balsamic vinegar
5 parts Per Me olive oil (or high-quality
  extra virgin olive oil)

## GARNISH

1 tablespoon aged balsamic vinegar
2 teaspoons toasted pistachio oil
  (100 percent)
2 tablespoons toasted and crushed
  pistachio nuts

To make the Shaved Beets: Peel and trim the beets. Using a mandolin or sharp knife, thinly slice crosswise and place each color in separate bowls of ice water for up to 1 day. Before serving, dry well and then toss with oil, chives, salt, and pepper.

To make the Salad: Clean, separate, and dry lettuces and sorrel. Refrigerate lightly covered with a paper towel until ready to plate.

To make the Vinaigrette: Dissolve salt in the vinegar and slowly whisk in oil until smooth. Add pepper and whisk or shake well before each use.

How to Plate: Toss Baby and Roasted Beets (red and yellow separately) in the Vinaigrette. Artfully arrange Roasted Beets on a chilled plate and top with Baby Beets interspersed with the Shaved Beets. Place lettuce and 3 to 4 sorrel leaves around the beets. Alternate drops of balsamic vinegar and pistachio oil around beets. Garnish with toasted pistachios and Beet Chips.

# Potato and Leek "Risotto" with Chanterelles and Spinach

8 SERVINGS

## MUSHROOM STOCK

2 tablespoons olive oil

2 shallots, diced

½ cup dried porcini mushrooms

1 cup fresh shiitake mushrooms

1 cup fresh chanterelles (include scraps and stems)

1 cup white wine

3 bunches fresh thyme

2 quarts water

## "RISOTTO"

1 pound fresh leeks (white part only)

¼ cup olive oil

3 sprigs fresh thyme, tied in a bouquet

3 pounds large russet potatoes

2 quarts Mushroom Stock (recipe above)

2 cups dry white wine

4 cups spinach leaves

Salt and pepper to taste

## MUSHROOM GARNISH

2 cups chanterelle mushrooms

2 tablespoons olive oil

1 cup white shimeji or shiitake mushrooms

Salt and pepper to taste

1 tablespoon minced chives

To make the Mushroom Stock: Heat a large heavy saucepan over medium heat. Add oil and shallots. Cook shallots until translucent. Add mushrooms and coat well with oil. Deglaze with the wine and add thyme. Reduce until wine glazes and then add water. Simmer for 30 minutes and remove from heat. Allow mushrooms to infuse the water for 10 minutes. Strain through a fine mesh sieve, reserving liquid. Chill until needed.

To make the "Risotto": Thinly slice the leeks crosswise into semi-circles. Rinse well under cold running water until clear of dirt; drain well and remove any excess water. Heat oil in a heavy pot over low heat. Add leeks and cook slowly until translucent. Add thyme bouquet. Season lightly and coat well with additional oil. Cook for 8 to 10 minutes. As leeks are cooking, peel potatoes, slice into ⅛-inch slices and then into ⅛-inch dice. Do not place the potatoes in water. Toss them lightly in a thin coat of oil. (Placing them in water would drain off essential starch needed to thicken the dish.) In a separate pot, simmer Mushroom Stock.

Add potatoes to the cooking leeks and coat well. Stir consistently for 3 minutes or so. Deglaze with wine and reduce until dry, continuing to stir. Ladle enough simmering stock to just cover potatoes. Continue to stir as potatoes simmer and stock is absorbed. Once stock is absorbed, add more stock to cover, continue to stir until mixture reduces; repeat process once more, or until the potatoes are thoroughly tender and cooked. Julienne the spinach leaves. As mixture begins to thicken, add spinach and wilt until smoothly incorporated into the potatoes. The mixture should appear creamy and thick from the starch released from the potatoes. Adjust seasoning and prepare to serve.

## MUSHROOM GARNISH

2 cups chanterelle mushrooms

2 tablespoons olive oil

1 cup white shimeji or shiitake
    mushrooms

Salt and pepper to taste

1 tablespoon minced chives

To make the Mushroom Garnish: Clean and rinse the chanterelles in cold running water and drain well on a clean cloth to remove all excess liquid. Moments before serving, heat a heavy sauté pan with oil over high heat and allow to smoke lightly. Add mushrooms, sautéing briefly until tender. Finish with salt, pepper, and chives. Keep warm until needed.

How to Plate: Divide the "Risotto" into warm pasta bowls. Top with the Mushroom Garnish.

# Caramelized Silken Tofu "Brûlée" with Marinated Strawberries

8 SERVINGS

## STRAWBERRY SORBET

4 cups fresh puréed strawberries
   (about 2½ pounds whole berries)
1 cup light corn syrup
1 teaspoon white balsamic vinegar
⅛ teaspoon salt

## STRAWBERRY SAUCE

6 pints strawberries (about 3 pounds),
   rinsed, hulled, and quartered
3 vanilla beans
2 cups sugar
2 tablespoons balsamic vinegar
2 tablespoons grenadine syrup
¼ cup fresh lemon juice
1 cup white wine

## MINT OIL

2 small bunches mint
½ cup vegetable oil

## CARAMELIZED TOFU

2 (12- to 16-ounce) packages
   silken tofu, extra firm
¼ cup sugar

## PULLED SUGAR GARNISH

8 ounces isomalt
¼ cup water
Red dye paste

To make the Strawberry Sorbet: Fill 3 to 4 layers of cheesecloth with puréed strawberries (in small batches). Over a bowl, strain strawberries by gathering corners of cheesecloth together, and twist and squeeze from the top. Combine all ingredients in a bowl and follow the directions of your ice cream maker.

To make the Strawberry Sauce: Place all ingredients in a pot over medium-low heat. Simmer until strawberries become opaque in color. Strain while not pushing strawberries through, as you want a clear liquid. Chill sauce until ready to use.

To make the Mint Oil: Rinse and pick mint leaves; blanch and chill. Remove excess water from the mint and place in a blender. Slowly add the oil and blend until oil starts to warm. Remove and strain through a cheesecloth. Set aside until plating.

To make the Carmelized Tofu: Slice tofu to desired size. Generously top with sugar and caramelize using a pastry torch.

To make the Pulled Sugar Garnish: Combine all ingredients in a heavy pan and cook to 330 degrees F on a candy thermometer. Pour mixture onto Silpat. Using a spatula, fold mixture into middle of Silpat until you can pick it up while wearing neoprene gloves; work into a ball by constantly folding outside edges towards the middle. While still pliable but not too soft, pull into ribbons and free-hand twist for garnish.

NOTE: Sugar cannot be substituted for the isomalt. Other sugar-based recipes can be sought to make a similar garnish.

## STRAWBERRY GARNISH

1 pint strawberries, rinsed, hulled,
   and diced

How to Plate: Place the Caramelized Tofu on a dinner plate, spoon Strawberry Garnish on top and at various areas of the plate. Drizzle the Strawberry Sauce freely around the base of the tofu and the Mint Oil around the perimeter of the plate. Carefully place a scoop of the Strawberry Sorbet on top and prop the Pulled Sugar Garnish so that it stands over the sorbet.

# Anne Quatrano

*"Vegetables are the heart and soul of Southern cooking, even without the meat. They are the staff of sustenance."*

Anne Quatrano redefined Atlanta's dining scene when she and husband, Cliff Harrison, opened Baccanalia in 1993. Its daily prix fixe menus using seasonal dishes in a farmhouse quickly gained national media attention, and she eventually became known as the "Alice Waters of the Southeast." *Gourmet* has named Baccanalia one of its Top Tables, *Food & Wine* named the pair Best New Chefs of 1995, and an Atlanta Journal's four-star review rated the restaurant "perfection." Fourteen years later, the husband-and-wife cooking team continues to accumulate accolades and garner new awards, including Atlanta's top Zagat Survey rating and the James Beard Foundation Best Chef: Southeast.

Anne Quantrano attended California Culinary Institute in San Francisco and met her husband while in school. They worked their way down the East Coast from Nantucket and Manhattan and, in 1992, moved to Cartersville, Georgia, to renovate a farm that had been in her family for five generations. In 1993, they opened Baccanalia, using their culinary training and homegrown vegetables to set their menus apart from other local dining establishments. Today, Baccanalia is in a larger location, and the couple also runs Floataway Cafe and Star Provisions, a cook's market.

# Bruschetta with Avocado, Heirloom Tomatoes, and Basil

1 ripe avocado (about 8 ounces)

3 tablespoons fruity extra virgin
  olive oil (French, if possible)

Juice of 1 small lemon or
  ½ large lemon

Salt and pepper to taste

4 slices rustic sourdough bread

1 clove garlic, peeled and halved

3 to 4 heirloom tomatoes, depending
  on size

## GARNISH

Red onion, sliced and separated

Purple basil

Peel avocado and roughly mash it with a fork, adding 1 teaspoon olive oil or so, based on an 8-ounce avocado, to a guacamole texture. Add lemon juice. Season with salt and pepper.

Toast bread over an open fire or in a broiler. Brush with olive oil and rub with cut side of garlic. Place 1 slice of bread on each of four plates and then spread with avocado mash.

Slice and cube the tomatoes. Arrange around and on top of avocado mash; drizzle with remaining olive oil and season tomatoes with salt and pepper. Garnish with red onion and torn bits of purple basil.

# Crispy Fried Okra and Chiles with Pepper Vinegar

SERVES 4

½ cup okra, cut into ½-inch rounds

1 cup boiling water

1 cup all-purpose flour

1 tablespoon cornstarch

Salt and pepper to taste

3 cups peanut oil

1 pound okra, trimmed and cut in
half lengthwise

½ pound assorted small whole chiles
(banana pepper, Tabasco pepper,
and Thai chile, or any favorite small
chiles), stems trimmed

Pepper vinegar, for dipping (use store-
bought or recipe below)

## PEPPER VINEGAR

Hot peppers (about 6 ounces) to fill
a 1-pint wide-mouthed jar

1½ cups distilled white vinegar or
apple cider vinegar

Place ½ cup okra rounds into a stainless strainer over a bowl. Pour the boiling water over okra and let strain through, reserving the juice. Cool to room temperature.

In another bowl, mix flour, cornstarch, salt, and pepper; set aside.

In a large heavy saucepan, heat peanut oil to 350 degrees F. While the oil is heating, dip okra halves in the okra juice and then dredge in the flour mixture, shaking off any excess flour.

Fry okra halves until crispy (note that the okra might float before they are crispy); set aside. Fry the whole chiles until wrinkled; set aside. The chiles can be fried with the okra, if desired.

To make the Pepper Vinegar: Sterilize a heavy pint jar and lid by boiling in water. Wash and dry the fresh hot peppers. Choose your favorite red and/or green chile peppers (Scotch Bonnets or habañeros work well for this). A good distilled white vinegar is often used, but some prefer apple cider vinegar. Fill jars about three-fourths full with peppers and cover with vinegar to ½ inch from the top. Wipe the rim of the jar and cap tightly. Allow to stand for 2 to 3 weeks before using and up to 6 months in the refrigerator.

How to Plate: Distribute the okra and chiles onto four dinner plates, arranging them in a mound. Serve the Pepper Vinegar in small individual bowls for dipping.

# Summer Vegetable Pilaf with Carolina Gold Rice

SERVES 4

## TOMATO WATER

Tomato scraps, or 1 to 2 large
    tomatoes

## SUMMER VEGETABLES

6 cups water

1 cup shelled butter beans (if
    unavailable, use canned)

1 cup pink-eyed peas (can substitute
    black-eyed peas)

1 small summer squash, sliced
    into rounds

1 tablespoon olive oil

1 small sweet onion, diced

1 clove garlic, thinly sliced

2 sprigs fresh marjoram

1 cup fresh corn, cut off the cob
    (can substitute frozen)

1 teaspoon white wine or sherry
    vinegar

1 large heirloom tomato, diced

2 cups Tomato Water (recipe above)

Salt and pepper to taste

2 cups cooked Carolina Gold Rice
    (if unavailable, use another long
    grain rice)

To make the Tomato Water: Dice tomatoes, saving all the juice, and tie in a cheesecloth; let tomatoes drip over a bowl in the refrigerator for a day or so. If cheesecloth is not handy, use a sieve over a bowl. Reserve juice.

To make the Summer Vegetables: Heat the water in a stainless pot seasoned with some salt. Blanch each vegetable in the same water separately, and then shock by submerging in an ice bath; reserve the vegetables.

In a saucepan, heat most of the oil over medium heat. In the following order add the onion, garlic, 1 sprig marjoram, and corn. Cook for a few minutes, or until wilted but not colored. Add the vinegar, butter beans, pink-eyed peas, and squash. Cook for a few minutes for flavors to meld. Add tomato and Tomato Water. Season with salt and pepper.

How to Plate: Spoon vegetables over individual bowls of warm rice, add a few leaves of marjoram, and drizzle with remaining oil to serve.

# Cantaloupe Truffle Bar with Soy Caramel and Spearmint Ice

SERVES 4

*Luis Vasquez, Pastry Chef*

## SPEARMINT ICE

1 cup sugar

2 cups water

1 bunch spearmint leaves

## CHOCOLATE BAR AND CAGE STRIPS

8 ounces semisweet chocolate (dairy-free)

Chocolate transfer sheet

## GRANOLA BAR

8 small or 4 large dried pitted dates (4 ounces), diced

½ cup chopped toasted hazelnuts

## CHOCOLATE GANACHE

½ cup (about 3 ounces) bittersweet chocolate

2 tablespoons light corn syrup

½ cup soy milk

## SOY CARAMEL SAUCE

½ cup sugar

2 tablespoons corn syrup

1 cup soy milk

3 tablespoons water

1 teaspoon cornstarch

**To make the Spearmint Ice:** Place sugar in a saucepan. Blend the water and spearmint together and then add to the saucepan; simmer for 3 to 5 minutes; strain. Pour into a shallow stainless pan and freeze. Stir with a fork every hour for 4 hours. Fluff with a fork before serving.

**To make the Chocolate Bar and Cage Strips:** Melt chocolate in a double boiler with a tempering thermometer, positioned so that it does not touch the bottom of the pan, until it reaches 130 degrees F. Remove from the heat and cool down to 85 degrees F, stirring constantly. Allow ample time for this process, perhaps 30 minutes.

NOTE: Stirring over ice can shorten the process, but stirring must be constant and care taken to avoid any water coming into contact with the chocolate. Note that even the slightest amount of water will seize the chocolate and make it unusable.

Carefully heat chocolate again over the double boiler to a working temperature of 90 degrees F. (Note that this takes about 15 seconds—be careful not to heat over 90 degrees F or the chocolate will lose temper and you'll have to restart the process. To test if the chocolate is tempered, using a spatula, spread a very thin layer of chocolate over parchment paper. If it sets after 3 to 5 minutes, is dry to the touch, and presents a smooth shiny surface, it is tempered. If not, simply reheat to 130 degrees F and repeat the entire process.

Cut the transfer sheet to about 8 x 4 inches for the cage strips and place on parchment paper or a silicone mat with rough side of print facing up. Allow enough additional space for the chocolate bases that will not use the transfer sheet. With an offset spatula, spread a thin ⅛-inch layer of chocolate over the sheet and an area about 3 x 4 inches

*Recipe continued on page 30*

for the bases. Allow to set but only until somewhat firm and still flexible, about 5 to 10 minutes. Quickly cut the strips of chocolate for the cage into ¼ x 4-inch strips and then drape over a handle of a large spoon or a small rolling pin to make the desired shape for the cage. Cut four rectangles for the chocolate bar bases measuring 3 x 1 inches; set aside.

To make the Granola Bar: Combine dates and hazelnuts in a bowl. Place half the mixture in a food processor, process until sticky and holds together when pressed. Return to the bowl and combine with the other half of the dates and hazelnuts. Press this mixture into a flat rectangle and place it between two sheets of parchment paper. Roll to ¼ inch thick and cut into four rectangles 3 x 1 inches; set aside.

To make the Chocolate Ganache: Coarsely chop the chocolate and place in a bowl with the corn syrup. Heat soy milk to a simmer and pour over the chocolate. Stir until chocolate is completely melted; set aside.

To make the Soy Caramel Sauce: In a small heavy-bottomed saucepan, cook sugar and corn syrup until it reaches an amber color. In a small bowl, combine soy milk, water, and cornstarch. Pour this mixture very gradually into the caramelized sugar mixture and whisk until thick. If the mixture becomes thick quickly and is difficult to stir, continue heating and stirring until a sauce consistency occurs; cool.

MELON BALLS

1 cantaloupe

GARNISH

4 fresh mint sprigs
Sea salt
Cacao nibs

To make the Melon Balls: Cut cantaloupe in half and remove seeds. Using a small-sized melon baller, scoop enough balls to make about 1 cup.

How to Plate: Place a Chocolate Bar on each dinner plate. Top each with a Granola Bar and add two rows of Melon Balls. Make a line of Chocolate Ganache in the center of the melon balls the length of the dessert. Top with 6 bent chocolate strips evenly spaced to create the cage, attaching to the chocolate base at the bottom edges.

Attach cage strips by holding a knife under hot water and dry completely. Quickly touch the ends of the cage strips to the knife to create a "glue" and attach to the chocolate bar base. Adjust the length of the strips as needed.

Using a large spoon, drizzle Soy Caramel Sauce along the side of the chocolate bar in the center of the plate.

Fill a small chilled glass with the Spearmint Ice and top with a sprig of mint. Set on opposite side of the plate. Garnish plate with sea salt and cacao nibs.

# Bradford Thompson

*"Preparing special vegan dishes was difficult at first and a challenge. Now, I am rethinking the way I cook. I realized that by using one ingredient in a few preparations, I could create layers of flavor and texture."*

Bradford Thompson creates luxurious French food with a modern edge using the highest quality ingredients. Growing up in New England, his summers on the coast of Maine ignited a culinary passion and his aspiration to become one of the top chefs in the country. After several years at Max-a-Mia and Max-on-Main in Hartford, Connecticut, he moved west to Phoenix to work under award-winning chef Vincent Guerithault at Vincent's on Camelback. He learned classic French cooking with a southwestern twist and continued to pursue career-defining tutelages with celebrated chef Alex Stratta at Mary Elaine's at the Phoenician and legendary chef Daniel Boulud.

Thompson's five years with chef Daniel Boulud in New York included working on two cookbooks, opening Café Boulud and DB Bistro Moderne, and handling private dining for Restaurant Daniel. Thompson has been featured on the Food Network, *The Today Show,* and in *Gourmet, Bon Appétit,* the *New York Times,* and the *Wall Street Journal.* After leaving New York, he returned to Phoenix to take the helm at Mary Elaine's and scored some of the most coveted industry awards such as the prestigious AAA Five-Diamond award and the Mobile 5-star award, and where he was named one of the ten Best New Chefs in *Food & Wine* magazine in 2004. In 2005, he was named Outstanding Chef of the Year by Share Our Strength; in 2006, he was inducted into the Scottsdale Culinary Hall of Fame and named James Beard Foundation Best Chef: Southwest.

# Celery Root Soup and Celery Apple Salad with Almonds

SERVES 6 TO 8

## CELERY ROOT SOUP

1½ whole onions, thinly sliced

1 tablespoon olive oil

1 leek, rinsed and thinly sliced

1 cup thinly sliced fennel

3 cloves garlic, thinly sliced

Salt and pepper to taste

1 russet potato, thinly sliced

3 pounds celery root, peeled and diced

1 quart vegetable stock

2 cups almond milk, plain and unsweetened

## CELERY ROOT SALAD

2 heads celery root, 2 cups grated with remainder diced for purée

1 (13.5-ounce) can coconut milk

1 green apple, grated

Salt and pepper to taste

¼ cup crushed Marcona almonds

## GARNISHES

Celery root, sliced into paper-thin rounds and fried in 325-degree F oil until lightly browned

½ cup apple butter

Celery leaves

1 green apple, unpeeled and julienned (see note)

¼ cup Marcona almonds, coarsely crushed

To make the Celery Root Soup: In a large heavy-bottomed saucepot, sweat the onions in oil until tender. Add leek, fennel, and garlic, continuing to sweat until soft. Season with salt and pepper. Add potato, celery root, and vegetable stock. Cook over medium heat for 1 hour, or until tender. Add almond milk and remove from heat; allow to sit for about 10 minutes. Transfer mixture to a blender and blend until smooth. Adjust seasoning to taste.

To make the Celery Root Salad: Place diced celery root and coconut milk into a heavy ziplock freezer bag and seal tightly. Place in a pot of simmering water (about 150 degrees F) and cook, covered, over low heat for 2 hours, or until tender; cool slightly. Remove celery root mixture from bag and purée in a high-speed blender, adding just enough coconut milk to create a smooth purée; set aside.

Blanch grated celery root and apple for 1 minute; drain and cool immediately in ice water. Drain again. Add purée to apple and celery root mixture to a desired consistency. Season with salt and pepper. Mix in almonds before serving.

How to Plate: Serve Celery Root Soup in a demitasse and top with a few of the fried celery root chips. Place cup on one side of a thin rectangular plate. Spread a spoonful of apple butter across the opposite side of the plate and place a quenelle of the Celery Root Salad on top. Garnish with celery leaves, julienned apple, and almonds.

NOTE: To keep apple from browning, sprinkle julienned strips with vitamin C powder or lemon juice.

# Baby Beet Salad with Pistachio Vinaigrette and Chickpea Fritters

SERVES 4

## BABY BEETS

Kosher salt

6 baby red beets

6 baby yellow beets

6 baby Chioggia beets

## PISTACHIO VINAIGRETTE

4 tablespoons fennel purée (cook
fennel in water and then purée)

1 tablespoon pistachio paste

2 tablespoons grapeseed oil

1 tablespoon walnut oil

1 tablespoon sherry vinegar

Salt and pepper to taste

To make the Baby Beets: Line a small baking dish with salt. Peel beets and trim the tops and bottoms. (Save beet skins and scraps for the Borscht Coulis.) Wrap beets by color into a piece of foil and place foil packages into baking dish. Roast at 325 degrees F for about 40 minutes, or until tender. Remove from oven and peel the skins from the beets. Reserve the beets until ready to use.

To make the Pistachio Vinaigrette: Whisk all ingredients together in a large mixing bowl until well combined. Check seasoning and adjust. Blend with an immersion blender to emulsify.

## BEET CHIPS

1 large unpeeled red beet

1 large unpeeled yellow beet

Simple syrup (3 parts hot water to
    1 part sugar, dissolved and cooled)

## BORSCHT COULIS

1 cup beet scraps (add diced beets
    if needed to fill cup)

1 tablespoon olive oil

Salt and pepper to taste

1 cup water

1 sachet made of fennel seeds, cumin,
    and peppercorns

1 cup red beet juice

## PICKLED ONIONS

1 large red onion, thinly sliced

2 tablespoons sugar

8 tablespoons rice wine vinegar

1 sachet made of 1 teaspoon mustard
    seed, 1 teaspoon fennel seed,
    1 dried chile, 2 teaspoons black
    pepper, and 2 teaspoons coriander

## CHICKPEA FRITTERS

8 ounces chickpea flour

1 quart water

Salt and pepper to taste

2 tablespoons olive oil

Cornstarch/cold water slurry (thin
    paste, 1 to 2 ratio)

Panko breadcrumbs

## GARNISH

Pistachio shavings for dusting
    (shaved on a microplane)

Bibb lettuce leaves, rinsed and
    patted dry

Cumin seeds

To make the Beet Chips: Slice each color of beet into paper-thin circles. Dip beet slices in simple syrup and lay out on a Silpat-lined baking sheet. Bake at 225 degrees F for 1 hour, or until dry and crispy. Store in an airtight container lined with paper towels.

To make the Borscht Coulis: In a medium saucepan, sweat beet scraps in olive oil and season with salt and pepper. Add the water and sachet, and cook, covered, over low heat until tender. When cooked, remove sachet from pan and place beets in a blender. Blend on low speed until smooth and then pass through a strainer. When cooled, whisk in beet juice until consistency is still thick but smooth enough to spread. Adjust seasonings and set aside.

To make the Pickled Onions: Blanch onion in salted water for 2 minutes; drain well and place into a medium-size bowl. In a saucepan, boil remaining ingredients, pour boiled mixture onto onion, and allow to cool at room temperature.

To make the Chickpea Fritters: Whisk the chickpea flour and water together until smooth; season with salt and pepper. Pour into a saucepan and slowly bring the heat up, stirring constantly, until the mixture comes together and is cooked, about 20 minutes; adjust seasonings. Add the oil and whisk with a few strokes until just combined. Pour mixture onto a baking sheet lined with parchment paper and allow to cool overnight in the refrigerator. The next day, cut into squares, dip into the cornstarch paste and then into panko breadcrumbs to coat. Refrigerate until ready to fry. Fry in hot oil (350 degrees F) for 1 1/2 to 2 minutes, or until brown.

How to Plate: On a large plate, create a scant pool of Pistachio Vinaigrette on a third of the plate. Arrange Baby Beets, alternating colors onto pool. Intersperse the red and yellow Beet Chips with the Baby Beets. Garnish with pistachio shavings. Use a piece of Bibb lettuce leaf to create a "cup" next to the beets. Place Pickled Onions on top and a couple of Chickpea Fritters on the side. Spread a line of Borscht Coulis across the plate. Garnish strip with cumin seeds.

# Roast Vegetable Pot Pie

SERVES 4

## PIE CRUST

2 cups all-purpose flour

2 cups chickpea flour

2 teaspoons ground fennel seeds

2 teaspoons salt

½ cup water

½ cup olive oil

## VEGETABLES

16 baby carrots

8 baby turnips, halved and trimmed

8 baby leeks, rinsed and trimmed into
    2-inch pieces

8 Brussels sprouts, cut in half and
    blanched

Olive oil

Salt and pepper to taste

¼ to ½ cup water

1 cup Truffle Juice (recipe below)

4 pieces tomato confit, cut into quarters

## TRUFFLE JUICE

⅓ cup dried mixed mushrooms

1⅓ cups hot water

Salt and pepper to taste

## VEGETABLE PURÉE

2 shallots, thinly sliced

Olive oil

3 cloves garlic

1 large carrot, peeled and thinly sliced

1 sprig thyme

Salt and white pepper to taste

To make the Pie Crust: In a stand mixer fitted with a dough hook, add flours, fennel seeds, and salt. Mix at medium speed and alternately add water and oil until a ball starts to form. Remove from mixer. Knead dough by hand until smooth, wrap in plastic wrap, and refrigerate for at least 2 hours.

When ready to use, roll dough through a pasta machine until ⅛ inch thick; cut into ¾-inch strips. Working directly on a baking sheet lined with parchment paper or Silpat, make a lattice pattern with the strips and then cut with a ring cutter to the desired circumference, based on the size of the bowls in which the pot pies will be baked. Bake dough at 325 degrees F for 5 to 7 minutes and remove from oven. Brush with olive oil, and bake for another 5 to 7 minutes, or until golden.

To make the Vegetables: Cut and trim baby vegetables, reserving trimmings for the Vegetable Purée. Over low heat, cook the blanched Brussels sprouts, carrots, turnips, and leeks in just enough oil to lightly coat, and season with salt and pepper. Add the water and braise until tender. Add truffle juice and simmer 3 to 4 minutes. Drain vegetables and reserve all the cooking liquid for the Vegetable Purée. Add tomato confit to drained vegetables.

To make the Truffle Juice: Soak mushrooms in hot water for 15 to 20 minutes. Season with salt and pepper. Remove mushrooms.

To make the Vegetable Purée: In a large sauté pan, sweat the shallots in enough oil to coat until translucent. At the same time, blanch the garlic in boiling water. Add carrot to the shallots and continue to cook. Add garlic, reserved vegetable trimmings, and thyme. Season with salt and white pepper. Add the reserved cooking liquid plus ¼ cup water. Simmer until vegetables are tender. Adjust seasonings. Transfer entire contents to a blender and purée until smooth. Reserve the purée until ready to use.

## BLACK TRUMPET PURÉE

4 cups black trumpet mushrooms, washed very well and drained (other mushrooms may be used)

Olive oil

Salt and pepper to taste

½ cup port wine

¼ cup Truffle Juice (recipe on facing page)

## GARNISH

One small bunch sage leaves, fried in olive oil

To make the Black Trumpet Purée: In a large sauté pan over medium heat, cook mushrooms in a little oil and season with salt and pepper. Deglaze the pan with wine, and cook until dry. Add Truffle Juice and reduce slightly. Drain mushrooms and reserve the liquid. Put mushrooms in a blender and purée until smooth, drizzling the reserved liquid into the purée until incorporated. Adjust seasonings.

How to Plate: Warm the Vegetable Purée and divide among the bowls. Warm the Vegetables in a little water and olive oil until glazed and hot, and divide among the bowls, placing them into the purée. Top each dish with a Pie Crust. Drizzle with olive oil, then place a dollop of Black Trumpet Purée on top of the crust. Add a few pieces of fried sage on top to garnish.

# Coconut and Sweet Potato Custard, Pumpkin Seed Tuile, and Cinnamon Caramel

4 SERVINGS

## CARAMEL

(Make this 1 day ahead)

1 cinnamon stick, crushed

1/2 cup brown sugar

1/2 cup water

1/2 cup apple cider

## SIMPLE SYRUP

⅓ cup brown sugar

1 cup water

## SWEET POTATO CUSTARD

2 quarts water

2 cinnamon sticks

5 cloves

2 pounds sweet potatoes, peeled
   and cut into large dice

3 tablespoons agar-agar

2 (13.5-ounce) cans coconut milk

3 tablespoons Simple Syrup (recipe
   above)

## PUMPKIN SEED TUILE

1 pound store-bought prepared
   fondant

2 tablespoons glucose

2 tablespoons walnuts

6 tablespoons unsalted pumpkin
   seeds, divided

To make the Caramel: Place cinnamon stick and brown sugar in a heavy-bottom saucepan and cook over medium heat until sugar is a dark caramel; add water and cider. After the sugar seizes, adjust heat to low for 5 to 10 minutes to dissolve sugar completely, stirring constantly. Let caramel cool and set overnight on the counter. Next day, strain the liquid.

To make the Simple Syrup: Place sugar and a large spoonful of water into a heavy-bottom saucepan and cook over high heat until dark brown and well caramelized. Add the remaining water and simmer for 5 to 10 minutes until completely dissolved. Strain and reserve.

To make the Sweet Potato Custard: Set up a steamer basket or perforated pan over a steam bath of 2 quarts water, cinnamon sticks, and cloves. Place the sweet potatoes in the steamer basket and cook over medium heat for about 30 minutes, or until tender. Remove sweet potatoes and drain for a few minutes. Transfer to a blender or food processor. Meanwhile, combine agar-agar with coconut milk and simmer over low heat to dissolve, stirring frequently. Slowly add coconut milk mixture and Simple Syrup to sweet potato mixture and blend until very smooth. Pour into Flexipan or cupcake molds that have been sprayed with nonstick spray. Allow to set for 4 hours or overnight in the refrigerator.

To make the Pumpkin Seed Tuile: Combine fondant and glucose in a heavy-bottom saucepan and heat over medium heat until amber in color. Toss the nuts and 2 tablespoons pumpkin seeds into the mixture and stir to combine. Pour mixture onto a Silpat or parchment paper, and let cool completely. When cooled, crush to a powder in a food processor; sift. Form small circles of powder on a Silpat or parchment paper. Bake at 350 degrees F for 3 to 4 minutes. Allow to cool completely. Use remaining pumpkin seeds to garnish when plating.

How to Plate: Unmold custard directly onto serving plates. Pour Caramel over custard, forming a very shallow pool at the base. Artfully place pumpkin seeds around the custard and top with the Pumpkin Seed Tuile.

# Cat Cora

*"One of my first plant-based recipes was a mushroom pâté, and I loved every bite of it. How wonderful to enjoy pâté and still feel healthy. Cooking with plants forces more creativity and resourcefulness with the ingredients on hand."*

By the time she was fifteen, Cat Cora had already developed a business plan for her own restaurant. Raised in a small Greek community in Jackson, Mississippi, her first cookbook was inspired by her Greek and Southern heritage and included her favorite family recipes. Cat left Mississippi to attend the Culinary Institute of America in New York on the advice of her legendary mentor Julia Chef. After graduation, she worked at Arcadia with Anne Rozenweig and at Beekman Tavern with Larry Forgione of An American Place. Her culinary education continued in Europe as an apprentice with two of France's three-star Michelin chefs, George Blanc and Roger Verge, who taught her the cuisine of the French countryside and classical French cuisine.

Cora returned to New York as sous chef with Melissa Kelly at The Old Chatham Shepherding Company before planting her roots in northern California as chef de cuisine of Napa Valley's Bistro Don Giovanni. In 1999, Cora made her television debut as co-host of Food Network's *Melting Pot* with Rocco Di Spirito and, in 2005, she made television history as the first and only female Iron Chef on Food Network's *Iron Chef.* She is the president and founder of Chefs for Humanity, an emergency relief culinary community organization founded in response to the 2004 tsunami disaster. Cora also serves on the Macy's Culinary Council and is *Bon Appétit* magazine's executive chef. She is the author of two books, *Cat Cora Cooks* and *Cooking from the Hip: Fast Easy Phenomenal Meals.* In 2007, she opened her signature restaurant in California.

# Basque Veggie Kabobs with Key Lime Sauce

SERVES 6 TO 8

1 teaspoon sea salt

1 teaspoon freshly ground black
  pepper, or to taste

1 tablespoon dried orange rind

½ tablespoon chili powder

3 bell peppers, all colors, cut into
  2-inch pieces

1 red onion, cut into 8 pieces

2 portobello mushrooms, cut into
  quarters

2 zucchini, cut into 2-inch rounds

Olive oil

KEY LIME SAUCE

6 cloves garlic, peeled and chopped

3 dried bay leaves

1 fresh poblano pepper, coarsely
  chopped with the seeds left in

1 fresh serrano chile, coarsely
  chopped with the seeds left in

½ tablespoon sea salt

⅓ cup finely chopped fresh Italian
  flat-leaf parsley

¼ cup finely chopped fresh oregano

¼ cup finely chopped fresh basil

3 key limes

¼ cup sherry vinegar

⅓ cup olive oil

Combine salt, pepper, orange rind, and chili powder, and rub onto cut vegetables; set aside. Preheat a grill pan and soak some 10-inch wooden skewers in water.

To make the Key Lime Sauce: While vegetables are absorbing the rub, make the sauce by combining the garlic, bay leaves, peppers, and sea salt in a mortar and mash with a pestle until a smooth paste is formed. (If you do not have a mortar and pestle, put the ingredients in a blender with a teaspoon or so of vinegar.) Transfer paste to a mixing bowl and add the parsley, oregano, and basil. Juice the limes into the bowl. Whisk in the vinegar and oil until well combined; set aside.

Skewer the vegetables, layering by type and varying color, and grill on all sides until tender.

How to Plate: Arrange the kabobs on a large plate and drizzle with Key Lime Sauce. Use any remaining sauce as a dip.

# Curried Cauliflower with Currants and Pine Nuts

## DRESSING

¼ cup plus 2 tablespoons rice
   wine vinegar

1½ tablespoons granulated sugar

2 teaspoons Madras curry powder,
   or garam masala

¼ teaspoon sea salt

Freshly ground black pepper to taste

1/2 cup olive oil

## CAULIFLOWER

2 pounds cauliflower crowns

2 tablespoons kosher salt

1 cup pine nuts, toasted

1 cup dried currants

½ cup raw sunflower seeds

1 small red onion, finely chopped

## GARNISH

Cilantro leaves

To make the Dressing: In a large bowl, mix rice wine vinegar and sugar until the sugar is dissolved. Whisk in the curry powder, salt, and pepper. Very slowly, drizzle the olive oil and whisk into the vinegar mixture until incorporated. Taste and add more salt and pepper if desired; set dressing aside.

To make the Cauliflower: Blanch cauliflower in water with salt. Drain and add pine nuts, currants, sunflower seeds, and onion. Pour the dressing over the salad, tossing lightly to mix thoroughly. Chill for 1 to 2 hours before serving.

How to Plate: Mound salad onto plate in a pyramid shape. Garnish with a few cilantro leaves.

# Kiwi Parfait

SERVES 6

5 kiwis, peeled and cut into
   bite-size pieces
1 pint soy yogurt
1 cup crushed graham crackers
Curried Cashews (recipe below)

CURRIED CASHEWS
1 cup raw cashews
½ teaspoon canola oil
½ teaspoon curry powder
Salt to taste

Place a spoonful of kiwi pieces in the bottom of a martini glass. Top with soy yogurt to cover, and then add a layer of graham crackers. Notice how the layers are shaping from the outside of the glass. Repeat layers of kiwi and yogurt. Top with Curried Cashews and a few kiwi pieces.

To make the Curried Cashews: Preheat oven to 350 degrees F. Place cashews on an unlined baking sheet and bake for 12 minutes, or until fragrant and slightly browned. Toss nuts with canola oil and curry powder in a bowl. Add salt, if desired, and then cool.

# Charlie Trotter with Matthias Merges

*"For far too long vegetables have held a place on the back burner. As cuisiniers, we must hold the simple potato with the same reverence as we hold all parts of the meal."*

Charlie Trotter, one of the brightest stars of American gastronomy, is renowned for his innovative cuisine that embraces organically raised seasonal products. His brilliant flavor combinations are reflective of the more than ninety purveyors who provide fresh healthy ingredients that inspire his daily menus. Trotter began cooking professionally in 1982 after graduating from the University of Wisconsin with a degree in political science. He immersed himself for four years, working in Chicago, San Francisco, Florida, and Europe with chefs that included Norman Van Aken, Bradley Ogden, and Gordon Sinclair.

Charlie Trotter's restaurant is a member of the esteemed Relais & Chateaux and Traditions & Qualite. It has received five stars from the Mobil Travel Guide, five diamonds from AAA, and ten James Beard Foundation awards including Outstanding Restaurant. *Wine Spectator* has named it The Best Restaurant in the World for Wine & Food (1998) and America's Best Restaurant (2000). Trotter has won the IACP Humanitarian of the Year and been honored at the White House by Colin Powell's foundation *America's Promise* for his work. He is a member of the Board of Trustees of the James Beard Foundation, the author of fourteen cookbooks and two management books, and the host of an award-winning PBS cooking series, *The Kitchen Sessions with Charlie Trotter.*

**Matthias Merges,** corporate executive chef and service director for Charlie Trotter's Corporation, is a graduate of the Culinary Institute of America and has spent the past twelve years at Charlie Trotter's. He manages all restaurant and culinary operations under the Trotter "excellentist" plan including Charlie Trotter's Chicago, Restaurant C in Los Cabos, Mexico, Trotter's To-Go, and Charlie Trotter's Foods. He is also responsible for all cookbook development, television show content, and Trotter participation in special events.

# Warm Heirloom Tomatoes with Fava Beans and Crisp Squash Blossoms

SERVES 6

## TOMATOES

3 black tomatoes

3 yellow tomatoes

3 burgundy tomatoes

Sea salt

Grains of paradise, freshly ground,
  to taste

1 tablespoon finely chopped thyme

1 tablespoon finely chopped rosemary

1 tablespoon chives

¼ cup extra virgin olive oil, plus
  extra for drizzling

8 red currant tomatoes

8 yellow currant tomatoes

1 shallot, minced

## CRISP SQUASH BLOSSOMS

4 zucchini blossoms

2 cups grapeseed oil

Sea salt

Grains of paradise, freshly ground

## BASIL OIL

2 cups bush basil, whole leaf, loosely
  packed

3 tablespoons grapeseed oil, divided

To make the Tomatoes: Score the black, yellow, and burgundy tomatoes with an X on the bottom. Blanch quickly in boiling salted water until the skins begin to peel, and then immediately shock in ice water; remove skins and reserve tomatoes. Place tomato skins on a nonstick baking sheet or one lined with parchment paper and bake at 200 degrees F (convection oven at 175 degrees F) until skins are dehydrated and crispy, usually about 2 hours. When they are completely dried out, pulverize them in a coffee grinder, herb grinder, or small food processor; set aside.

Cut the tomatoes into quarters. Using a sharp knife, remove the seeds, creating a thick tomato "petal." Place all the tomato petals on a sheet tray and season liberally with sea salt, grains of paradise, thyme, rosemary, and chives. Finish with a generous drizzle of oil. Bake at 200 degrees F (convection at 170 degrees F) for approximately 1½ hours, or until half the moisture has evaporated.

Cut the currant tomatoes in half. Combine with shallot, ¼ cup oil, and sea salt; set aside.

To make the Crisp Squash Blossoms: Peel back zucchini blossom petals from core and stem. Deep fry the petals in 375-degree F grapeseed oil until crisp. Remove from oil and season with sea salt and grains of paradise. Reserve on paper towels to remove any residual oil.

To make the Basil Oil: Sauté basil in a hot sauté pan with 1 tablespoon grapeseed oil. Cool immediately by placing on paper towels in the refrigerator. When cold, combine basil and the remaining grapeseed oil in a blender until smooth. Pass through a coffee filter into a small container, letting the flavored oil slowly pass though the filter; set aside.

## FAVA BEANS

8 ounces fava beans, out of pod but not peeled

2 cups vegetable stock, divided

1 tablespoon extra virgin olive oil, plus more for seasoning

Sea salt and black pepper, freshly ground

1 tablespoon white wine vinegar

## GARNISH

½ cup micro basil, loosely packed

To make the Fava Beans: Blanch the fava beans in salted boiling water until tender. When cool enough to handle, peel shell from fava meat, split the bean in half, and remove the germ. Reserve half of the beans for plating. Place the remaining half of the favas in a blender with ¼ cup vegetable stock and the oil. Blend until smooth. Season with more oil, sea salt, pepper, and white wine vinegar.

How to Plate: Spoon the Fava Beans onto plates. Place two pieces of each kind of oven-dried tomato onto each sauced plate. Sprinkle marinated currant tomatoes on and around oven-dried tomatoes and sprinkle with micro basil. Place 4 to 6 pieces Crisp Squash Blossoms on plate. Drizzle remaining liquid from the currant tomatoes on the plates. Finish with a few drizzles of Basil Oil. Dust reserved tomato powder over all.

# Dusted Globe Artichokes with Water Mint, Pine Nut Butter, and Kinome Seeds

SERVES 4

## GLOBE ARTICHOKES AND VINAIGRETTE

1 teaspoon ground coriander seeds, divided

1 teaspoon ground fennel seeds, divided

1 teaspoon ground kinome seeds, divided

1 teaspoon chile flakes, divided

¼ cup extra virgin olive oil

2 tablespoons white wine vinegar

5 globe artichokes (4 for frying, 1 for sauce)

2 tablespoons arrowroot

¼ cup water

2 cups grapeseed oil, for frying

## MINT ARTICHOKE SAUCE

¾ cup water mint (can substitute other mints)

1 cup vegetable stock, divided

¼ cup extra virgin olive oil

Salt and pepper to taste

Juice of 2 lemons

## PINE NUT BUTTER

2 cups pine nuts

Vegetable stock

Salt and pepper to taste

White wine vinegar

To make the Globe Artichokes and Vinaigrette: Make a simple vinaigrette by combining half of each of the coriander, fennel seeds, kinome seeds, chile flakes, and the oil and vinegar; set aside.

Clean artichokes by removing leaves and leaving only peeled or "turned" core. Cook artichokes in a sealed bag in 193-degree F water until tender. Remove and cool to room temperature. Cut each artichoke in half and remove the flower. Then cut each half into quarters, reserving one whole artichoke for sauce. Liberally season the remaining four artichoke pieces with the remaining dry spices. Mix a slurry of arrowroot and ¼ cup water. Toss artichokes in slurry and fry in grapeseed oil at 375-degree F until crisp. Place on paper towels and set aside.

To make the Mint Artichoke Sauce: Blanch the water mint in unsalted water and then drain. Place in a blender with the reserved artichoke, ½ cup vegetable stock, and oil, puréeing until smooth. Season with salt, pepper, and lemon juice; set aside.

To make the Pine Nut Butter: Toast the pine nuts in a 280-degree F oven for 20 minutes, or until just golden brown. Purée half of the nuts with just enough vegetable stock to create a thick consistency. Season with salt and pepper and a splash of vinegar.

## WATER MINT OIL

¼ cup water mint (can substitute other mints)

1 teaspoon sugar

2 tablespoons olive oil

## GARNISH

Mint with stems cut short, 8 to 10 l per serving

1 teaspoon mint flowers per serving

Chile flakes

Kinome seeds

Pine nuts

To make the Water Mint Oil: Place water mint, sugar, and oil into a mortar and pestle. Grind until smooth and pass through a coffee filter into a small container; set aside.

How to Plate: Place ½ teaspoon of the Pine Nut Butter onto each plate. Drizzle Mint Artichoke Sauce over top. Divide the artichoke quarters on each plate and then top with mint. Finish with Mint Oil, mint flowers, chile flakes, kinome seeds, and pine nuts.

# Parslied Steel-Cut Oats with Turnip Confit, Chanterelle Mushrooms and Sage-Infused Red Wine Reduction

SERVES 4

## PARSLEY PURÉE

1 pound parsley

2 to 3 tablespoons extra virgin olive oil

## OATS

1 shallot, minced

1 clove garlic, minced

2 tablespoons extra virgin olive oil

2 cups steel-cut or rolled oats

1 quart vegetable stock, ½ cup reserved

Sea salt and pepper to taste

2 tablespoons sherry vinegar

## CHANTERELLE PURÉE

1 pound chanterelles

3 to 4 tablespoons olive oil

½ cup vegetable stock

## TURNIPS

8 tiny turnips

Extra virgin olive oil

Sea salt

Juice of 2 lemons

## PARSNIPS

8 ounces parsnips

2½ cups grapeseed oil

To make the Parsley Purée: In a blender, add parsley leaves and oil and blend until smooth; set aside.

To make the Oats: Sweat shallot and garlic in oil until translucent. Add oats and cook for 2 minutes before adding vegetable stock in small amounts at a time, as though cooking risotto style, until completely absorbed by oats and thoroughly cooked. Add Parsley Purée and finish with salt, pepper, and sherry vinegar.

To make the Chanterelle Purée: Sauté chanterelles in oil until soft. Reserve half for plating and purée the remaining half with reserved vegetable stock until smooth; set aside.

To make the Turnips: Clean the turnips and place in a medium-size saucepan. Cover with oil and cook slowly over low heat until tender. Cut turnips into quarters and caramelize in a sauté pan. Marinate turnips in sea salt and lemon juice; set aside.

To make the Parsnips: Peel and slice parsnips into very thin ribbons using a vegetable peeler. Fry in grapeseed oil at 375-degree F until crisp. Place on paper towels to drain.

SAGE-INFUSED
RED WINE REDUCTION

2 cups red wine for reduction,
perhaps Cabernet Sauvignon

GARNISH

2 tablespoons small tender thyme

To make the Sage-Infused Red Wine Reduction: Add red wine to a saucepan and bring to a boil. Reduce heat and simmer until reduced to about $1/2$ cup, about 20 minutes.

NOTE: A couple of weeks ahead, place some sage leaves into the desired wine and allow to steep.

How to Plate: Place Chanterelle Purée on a plate. Add a larger amount of the Oats next to the purée. Place the reserved mushrooms and Turnips on top of the purée. Sprinkle Parsnips and thyme around the plate. Garnish with dots of Red Wine Reduction.

# Raw Vanilla Bean Cheesecake with Mango, Shiso, and Allspice Vinaigrette

SERVES 4 TO 6

### SPICED CASHEWS

1 cup soaked raw cashews

3 tablespoons maple sugar

¼ teaspoon sea salt

¼ teaspoon ground Jamaican allspice

### DEHYDRATED MANGO CHIPS

1 ripe mango, peeled and cut
    into chunks

1 teaspoon ground Jamaican allspice

### RAW VANILLA BEAN
### CASHEW CHEESECAKE

2 cups soaked raw cashews

¼ cup lemon juice

¾ cup agave syrup

½ cup melted cocoa butter

¼ cup melted coconut butter

1 cup filtered water

2 vanilla beans, scraped

1 teaspoon psyllium husk powder

¼ teaspoon salt

### ALLSPICE VINAIGRETTE

½ cup white wine vinegar

2 tablespoons agave syrup

½ teaspoon ground Jamaican allspice

½ cup olive oil

Sea salt and black pepper

To make the Spiced Cashews: Combine cashews, maple sugar, salt, and allspice in a medium bowl, and toss evenly to coat. Spread the nuts on a nonstick drying sheet and place in the dehydrator at 105 degrees F for 24 hours, or until crisp. Store in an airtight container.

To make the Dehydrated Mango Chips: In a high-speed blender, purée mango and allspice until very smooth. Using an offset spatula, spread mango purée as thin as possible onto nonstick drying sheets of a dehydrator. Place the sheets onto the dehydrator and dry at 105 degrees F for about 24 hours, or until crisp. Break into small shards and store in an airtight container.

To make the Raw Vanilla Bean Cashew Cheesecake: Place all ingredients into a high-speed blender and process until very smooth. Pour mixture into an 8 x 8-inch pan and cover with plastic wrap; let set in refrigerator for 8 hours.

To make the Allspice Vinaigrette: Combine vinegar, syrup, and allspice in a small bowl. Slowly drizzle in the oil while whisking continuously. Add salt and black pepper to taste; reserve.

### CASHEW FRUIT GRANITÉ

1 cup cashew fruit purée (substitute mango purée, store-bought or homemade, recipe below)

2 tablespoons agave syrup

### MANGO PURÉE

1 large or 2 small mangoes, peeled, pitted, roughly cut

### GARNISH

1 mango, cut into small cubes

Micro shiso

Maple syrup

To make the Cashew Fruit Granité: Whisk together purée and agave syrup. Freeze in a shallow pan, scraping with a fork every 30 minutes until ice crystals have formed.

To make the Mango Purée: In a blender or food processor, purée mango pieces. If needed, add a teaspoon of water at a time until purée texture.

How to Plate: In a small bowl, lightly dress mango cubes with Allspice Vinaigrette. Spoon mixture onto a plate in a line, reserving juices. Using 2 tablespoons, scoop and mold cheesecake into two quenelle shapes and place on each end of the plate. Sprinkle Mango Chips and chopped Spiced Cashews over plate. Spoon Cashew Fruit Granité onto each end of the plate. Garnish dish with micro shiso and drizzle with remaining vinaigrette and maple syrup.

# Warm Venezuelan Chocolate Cake with Merlot-Infused Cherries, Lemon Bergamot, and Chocolate Gelato

SERVES 8 TO 10

## CHOCOLATE GELATO

1½ cups almond milk*

¾ cup chopped young Thai
   coconut meat (see note)

1 cup coconut water (from
   the Thai coconut)

¼ cup sucanat (natural granulated
   sugar cane)

¼ cup maple syrup

¼ cup cocoa powder

2 tablespoons coconut oil

¼ vanilla bean, split and scraped

*If almond milk is unavailable, make it by
blending 1 cup filtered water with ¾ cup
sliced raw almonds until silky smooth.

## CHOCOLATE OLIVE OIL CAKE

1½ cups cake flour

1 cup sucanat, finely ground
   in blender

¼ cup natural cocoa powder

2 teaspoons baking soda

1 teaspoon salt

2 tablespoons white wine vinegar

1 cup brewed coffee

1 vanilla bean, scraped (or 1 teaspoon
   vanilla extract)

¼ cup plus 1 tablespoon extra virgin
   olive oil

To make the Chocolate Gelato: In a high-speed blender, combine almond milk, coconut meat, coconut water, sugar, maple syrup, cocoa powder, oil, and vanilla bean seeds; process until smooth. Freeze in an ice cream maker according to the manufacturer's directions.

NOTE: It is important to learn how to open a Thai coconut and remove the meat. See page 199 for instructions.

To make the Chocolate Olive Oil Cake: Preheat oven to 350 degrees F. In a large mixing bowl, combine flour, sugar, cocoa powder, baking soda, and salt. In another bowl, whisk together vinegar, coffee, vanilla bean, and oil. Pour liquid ingredients into dry ingredients and whisk together until smooth. Pour into an oiled cake pan, Madeleine pan, mini cupcake pan, or readily available mini cupcake liners (using 2 teaspoons of batter each), and bake until the center of the cake springs back when touched, about 10 to 12 minutes. Set on cooling rack to cool.

NOTE: Makes about 2½ cups batter. If using mini cupcakes, the yield of 60 will be more than what is needed for the recipe. Extra can be frozen for future use.

*Recipe continued on next page*

## BITTERSWEET CHOCOLATE SAUCE

3½ ounces 70% dark chocolate

1 tablespoon corn syrup

2 tablespoons sugar

3 to 4 tablespoons water

## MERLOT-INFUSED SOUR CHERRIES

1 cup dried sour, or sweet dried
   cherries (like Bing)

3 cups Merlot or other red wine

2 tablespoons sugar

## GARNISH

Cacao nibs

Micro lemon bergamot

To make the Bittersweet Chocolate Sauce: Coarsely chop chocolate and place in a bowl. Add syrup and sugar to chocolate. Bring water to a boil. Pour about half over chocolate, whisking constantly, adding remainder of water as needed until the sauce is thick and smooth. Set aside.

To make the Merlot-Infused Sour Cherries: Place all ingredients in a saucepan. Bring to a boil and continue to cook for 5 minutes; strain and set aside. Continue to reduce the Merlot until it has a syrup-like consistency, about 20 to 30 minutes. Pour the syrup back onto the cherries and mix well.

How to Plate: Place 3 pieces or muffins of Chocolate Olive Oil Cake on a plate or shallow bowl. Spoon Merlot-Infused Sour Cherries around the cakes. Spoon Bittersweet Chocolate Sauce over the cakes and drizzle around the plate. Sprinkle plate with cacao nibs and spoon Chocolate Gelato in a small mound on the nibs. Garnish with micro lemon bergamot.

---

# *Mignardises*

MAKES APPROXIMATELY 80 PIECES (BASED ON SIZE)

1 cup raw cashew butter

1 cup maple syrup

1 cup cocoa powder

½ teaspoon vanilla seeds scraped
   from vanilla bean

1 tablespoon nama shoyu

Variety of coatings such as coconut,
   sesame seeds, crushed pumpkin
   seeds, cayenne pepper, or
   chopped dried fruit

In a food processor, combine all of the ingredients and process until smooth and thick. Pour into a shallow container and cover and refrigerate for 4 hours. Using a melon baller, scrape truffle base into small balls. Fill or roll chocolate truffles with spices, seeds, nuts, or dried fruits of your choice. Shape as desired (rounds, pear-shaped, nougat, or cylinders).

# Dan Barber

*"Cooking and eating with the seasons inspires more than it restricts—I think it might inspire because it restricts. If it's August, I'm inspired to use spring beans and would like to see them in one form or another on every dish. On every dish! They're perfect then, so that by the time fall squash finally comes, I want to be tired of eating beans. I want to be happy to see them go, thrilled to be done with them. I want to taste that first New York black dirt squash and smile like I just struck gold."*

Dan Barber's "haute organic" New American cuisine features fresh ingredients in nourishing and inventive menus. He first learned to respect seasonal locally grown produce while farming and cooking for family and friends at Blue Hill Farm in the Berkshires. Barber and Blue Hill gained a national reputation with a 3-star *New York Times* review and Barber being named one of the best new chefs in the country in 2002 in *Food & Wine* magazine. He has also been featured in *Gourmet,* the *New Yorker, Martha Stewart Living, Vanity Fair*'s 2007 Green Issue and in *Bon Appétit*'s "The Next Generation" of Great Chefs in its tenth annual restaurant issue. His op-ed pieces addressing local food systems and other writings have garnered him numerous Best Food Writing awards.

In 2004, Blue Hill at Stone Barns and The Stone Barns Center for Food and Agriculture opened its doors to focus on issues of pleasure, taste, and regional bounty. Barber has been an active advocate for sustainable agriculture and guided a passionate mission to create consciousness about the effects of everyday food choices. Both Blue Hill and Blue Hill at Stone Farms have received Best New Restaurant nominations from the James Beard Foundation, and Barber was named 2006 Best Chef: New York City. He serves on the Harvard Medical School's Center for Health and the Global Environment Advisory Board and continues to work with the Kellogg Foundation, New York's Green Markets, and Slow Food USA to minimize the political and intellectual rhetoric around agricultural policies and to promote the appreciation of good food.

# Tomato and Melon Salad with Tomato Sorbet

SERVES 4

BEEFSTEAK TOMATOES CONFIT

5 pounds beefsteak tomatoes

1 sprig thyme, stemmed

1 teaspoon sugar

1 clove garlic, sliced

2 tablespoons olive oil, plus more

Salt and pepper to taste

To make the Beefsteak Tomatoes Confit: Blanch tomatoes in boiling water for 30 seconds and then immediately plunge into an ice water bath. Using a knife, remove skins when cool enough to touch and then cut tomatoes in half and remove seeds. Place cut side down on a baking sheet and sprinkle with thyme, sugar, garlic, oil, salt, and pepper. Bake at 200 degrees F for 4 hours. Remove tomatoes from oven and transfer to a covered container. Cover with more olive oil and refrigerate until ready to serve.

## TOMATO SORBET

½ cup lemon juice

½ pound powdered sugar (or to taste)

1 cup mint, fine chiffonade

2 tablespoons finely chopped lemon thyme leaves or 1 tablespoon regular thyme

⅛ teaspoon salt

## TOMATO MELON SALAD

5 to 8 assorted and colorful heirloom tomatoes, sliced ¼ inch thick

2 tablespoons high-quality olive oil

1 tablespoon raspberry wine vinegar

1 tablespoon sherry vinegar

Salt and pepper to taste

½ cup honeydew melon, sliced to resemble tomatoes in size

½ cup cantaloupe, sliced to resemble tomatoes in size

½ cup watermelon, sliced to resemble tomatoes in size

## GARNISH

2 teaspoons green and purple opal basil, chiffonade

¼ cup thinly sliced sun-dried tomatoes

To make the Tomato Sorbet: Purée the Beefsteak Tomato Confit in a blender with lemon juice, powdered sugar, mint, thyme, and salt until smooth. Place mixture in an ice cream maker and follow the manufacturer's instructions. Freeze until ready to serve.

To make the Tomato Melon Salad: Chill serving bowls. Remove Tomato Sorbet from freezer to soften. Lay sliced tomatoes in a single layer and then drizzle with oil and vinegars; season with salt and pepper and set aside. Place melon slices in a very hot sauté or grill pan and sear for 20 seconds on one side only. Remove from pan.

How to Plate: Divide and place tomatoes, varying colors, at the bottom of chilled bowls. Stack with melon slices. Garnish by sprinkling with basil and sun-dried tomato slices. Top with a quenelle of Tomato Sorbet created by rolling a spoonful of sorbet between two large spoons.

# Summer Vegetables in Horseradish Vinaigrette

SERVES 4

## TOMATO WATER

15 large tomatoes

½ sweet bell pepper, any color, seeded

Tip of a serrano pepper, seeded

½ cucumber, peeled and seeded

2 teaspoons sugar

1 tablespoon vodka

⅛ teaspoon salt

To make the Tomato Water: Roughly chop tomatoes, peppers, and cucumber. Place all ingredients in a food processor and pulse to combine ingredients until slightly coarse. (You may need to process in batches depending on the size of your machine.) Line a large strainer with three or four layers of cheesecloth or an old cotton napkin, and place on top of a large bowl. Pour ingredients into strainer and allow liquid to drain overnight. Refrigerate or freeze up to 4 months.

NOTE: After straining is complete, use leftover tomatoes for sauces or spreads by combining with seasonings of your choice.

## TOMATO CONFIT

6 plum tomatoes

1 sprig thyme

1 teaspoon sugar

1 clove garlic, sliced

2 tablespoons olive oil, plus more

Salt and pepper to taste

## HORSERADISH VINAIGRETTE

1 tablespoon prepared horseradish

¾ teaspoon Dijon mustard

1 tablespoon tomato vinegar or
   champagne vinegar

½ cup high-quality olive oil

Salt and pepper to taste

## SUMMER VEGETABLES

2 baby yellow squash, thinly sliced

4 small apricots, pitted and quartered

½ cup haricots verts, blanched and
   cut into 1-inch pieces

½ cup yellow wax beans, cut in half
   and blanched

½ cup Hakurei turnips, cut into
   bite-size pieces and blanched

½ cup chanterelles, lightly sautéed

Salt and pepper to taste

To make the Tomato Confit: Blanch tomatoes in boiling water for 30 seconds and then immediately plunge tomatoes into an ice water bath. Using a knife, remove skins when cool enough to touch, cut tomatoes in half lengthwise, and remove seeds. Place cut side down on a baking sheet and sprinkle with thyme, sugar, garlic, oil, salt, and pepper. Bake at 200 degrees F for 4 hours. Remove from oven and transfer to a container. Cover tomatoes with olive oil and reserve in the refrigerator.

To make the Horseradish Vinaigrette: In a medium bowl, combine horseradish, mustard, and vinegar. Whisk in oil to make a loose vinaigrette. Season with salt and pepper.

To make the Summer Vegetables: Season each vegetable with salt and pepper.

How to Plate: Combine 1 quart Tomato Water and 1 tablespoon Horseradish Vinaigrette; season with salt and pepper. Divide Summer Vegetables and Tomato Confit among four chilled soup bowls by alternating type and color. Cover with Tomato Water mixture.

NOTE: This recipe will take overnight steps.

# Cauliflower Steak with Quinoa

SERVES 4

2 large heads cauliflower, cut into
   1-inch-thick steaks
Olive oil for coating and sautéing
Salt and pepper to taste
1 cup quinoa
1½ cups vegetable stock, divided
2 shallots, sliced
1 leek, rinsed and sliced (white
   part only)
1 small apple, peeled and diced
1 clove garlic, finely chopped
½ cup zucchini in ¼-inch dice
1 teaspoon finely chopped fresh
   thyme leaves
1 tablespoon finely chopped chives

BASIL OIL
2 cups well-washed basil leaves
1 cup grapeseed oil, chilled

At the largest part of each cauliflower head, cut two cross sections to create two 1-inch-thick steaks. In a large sauté pan coated with oil, brown the cauliflower steaks until golden brown on each side. Season with salt and pepper and set aside.

Over medium-low heat, sweat quinoa in 1 tablespoon oil until a nutty aroma is achieved. Turn off heat and add 1 cup stock; simmer until almost dry. Cover and let stand for 15 minutes. Fluff with a fork and set aside.

Cut remaining cauliflower into small florets and blanch in salted water until tender. Drain and spread florets on a baking sheet and place in a 300-degree F oven for about 15 minutes, or until florets have dried.

In a sauté pan, gently sweat the shallots, leek, apple, and garlic. Add the cauliflower florets and season with salt and pepper. Remove from heat, place in blender, and purée. (You will only need a few teaspoons for this recipe. The remaining purée can be frozen or thinned with stock for a cauliflower soup.) In a large sauté pan coated with oil, sauté zucchini until slightly golden brown. Add quinoa and remaining vegetable stock. Season with salt and pepper to taste. Add 2 teaspoons cauliflower purée to thicken, add thyme and chives, and drizzle with oil.

To make the Basil Oil: Blanche basil and then shock in ice water; dry leaves well. In a blender, purée basil and grapeseed oil; strain.

How to Plate: Place cauliflower steak on bed of quinoa and zucchini mixture and drizzle Basil Oil around the plate.

# Blueberry Compote and Peach Sorbet

SERVES 4

### BLUEBERRY COMPOTE

Juice of ½ lemon

½ cup water

¼ cup sugar

1 quart blueberries, rinsed

### PEACH SORBET

4 cups peach purée (fresh or frozen peaches puréed in a blender)

¼ cup simple syrup (boil ½ cup sugar with ¼ cup water)

6 tablespoons glucose or corn syrup

### GARNISH

1 tablespoon pineapple sage

To make the Blueberry Compote: Heat lemon juice, water, and sugar until the sugar dissolves. Stir in blueberries, remove from heat, and cool.

To make the Peach Sorbet: Combine ingredients and freeze in an ice cream maker according to the manufacturer's instructions. Freeze until ready to serve. You may have extra sorbet depending on serving size.

How to Plate: Spoon Blueberry Compote into four chilled bowls. Top with a scoop of Peach Sorbet. Garnish with pineapple sage chiffonade.

# Daniel Boulud

*"The better the soil, the better the soup!"*

Daniel Boulud's cuisine is rooted in the rhythm of the seasons and produce fresh from the fields of dedicated local purveyors. After apprenticeships in France and Copenhagen, Boulud came to Washington, D.C., as private chef to the European Commission. Soon after, he moved to New York, opening the Polo Lounge at the Westbury Hotel and Le Regence at the Plaza Athenee. In 1986, he became executive chef at Le Cirque and won Best Chef: New York City at the 1992 James Beard awards.

In 1993, Boulud opened Daniel, which was named "one of the top ten restaurants in the world" by the *Herald Tribune.* James Beard awarded Boulud Outstanding Chef of the Year, the *New York Times* gave Daniel four stars, and he was named Chef of the Year by *Bon Appétit* magazine. In 2006, Boulud was named Outstanding Restaurateur at the James Beard awards. Boulud's energy, creativity, and personal attention to detail as a restaurateur, author of numerous books, most recently *Braise: A Journey Through International Cuisine,* and creator of kitchenware and gourmet products are exceeded only by his generosity and deep humanity. He has served on the board of Citymeals-on-Wheels since 1999 and has hosted galas and raised funds for many other charitable causes.

He is the chef-owner of six award-winning restaurants: Daniel, Cafe Boulud, DB Bistro Modern, Bar Boulud in Manhattan, Cafe Boulud in Palm Beach, and Daniel Boulud Brasserie at Wynn Las Vegas Resort.

# Chilled Apple Consomme with Celery Root Rémoulade

SERVES 6

### APPLE CONSOMME

2 stalks celery

10 Granny Smith apples

2 teaspoons vitamin C powder
   or 2 tablespoons lemon juice

1 tablespoon apple pectin per
   3 cups of liquid (optional)

Salt and freshly ground white pepper
   to taste (optional)

To make the Apple Consomme: Cut celery and unpeeled apples into 1-inch chunks. Using a juicing machine, juice apples and celery together. Discard the waste and pass juice through a fine-mesh sieve. Whisk the vitamin C powder or lemon juice into the juice. If using apple pectin, use one-fourth of the apple and celery juice and whisk into the apple pectin. Bring mixture to a boil, whisking constantly until dissolved. Remove from heat and chill immediately. Once cold, whisk it back into the rest of the juice. This will give the consommé a slightly viscous quality. If desired, season the juice with salt and pepper to taste.

## CELERY ROOT RÉMOULADE

1 celery root, peeled and cut into fine
    julienne
2 tablespoons dairy-free mayonnaise
2 teaspoons Dijon mustard
2 tablespoons chopped chives
2 tablespoons chopped parsley
Salt and freshly ground white pepper
    to taste

## GARNISH

2 large celery root, peeled and
    cut into 60 battonets
    (2 x ¼ x ¼-inch-long pieces)
¼ cup celery root, peeled and
    finely diced
Olive oil
Salt and pepper to taste
1 cup picked celery leaves
⅓ cup shaved red radish (preferably
    using a mandoline)
¼ cup red apple (Macintosh or Gala)
    unpeeled, cut into brunoise
1 Granny Smith apple, unpeeled,
    half cut into fine julienne, half
    cut into brunoise

To make the Celery Root Rémoulade: Blanch celery root for about 15 seconds (reserve blanching water) and then shock in an ice water bath (reserve ice water). Drain the julienne and pat dry. The julienne should be cooked through but not falling apart. In a medium-size bowl, mix together the cooked celery root julienne, mayonnaise, mustard, chives, and parsley. Add salt and pepper; set aside.

How to Plate: Cook celery root battonets in the reserved blanching water for about 2 minutes, or until tender but not falling apart. Remove from water (reserve blanching water) and shock in reserved ice water; drain (reserve ice water). Cook celery root brunoise in reserved boiling water for about 10 seconds. Remove from water and shock in reserved ice water; drain and set aside.

Season celery root battonets with a bit of oil, salt, and pepper. Place 9 celery root battonets in a triangular shape on the bottom of six chilled bowls. On the inside of each triangle, pour enough Celery Root Remoulade to fill to the top. Garnish with celery leaves and red radish shavings. Pour about ⅓ cup Apple Consommé into the bottom of each bowl, around the celery root triangle. Sprinkle about 2 tablespoons each of the celery root brunoise, red apple brunoise, and Granny Smith apple brunoise into each bowl. Scatter the Granny Smith apple julienne on top of each dish as a final garnish. Serve immediately.

# Beet Salad with Red Beet Reduction, Walnut Chutney, Arugula, and Horseradish

SERVES 6

### BEET SALAD

2 pounds large red beets

2 pounds large yellow beets

2 tablespoons salt

2 tablespoons olive oil

2 tablespoons sherry vinegar

Salt and white pepper to taste

### BEET REDUCTION

1 pound large red beets, peeled

### WALNUT CHUTNEY

2 cups walnuts, shelled

1 tablespoon olive oil

⅓ cup walnut oil

1 tablespoon maple syrup

½ teaspoon sherry vinegar

½ teaspoon mustard powder

Salt and freshly ground pepper
  to taste

### CROUTONS

½ loaf slightly stale, unsliced
  white bread

1 tablespoon olive oil

Salt and freshly ground white
  pepper to taste

**To make the Beet Salad:** Wash red and yellow beets in cold water; place each color in separate pots and cover with cold water. Add 1 tablespoon salt to each pot and heat on high until boiling. Reduce to a simmer for 1 hour, or until tender. Drain, peel, and cut into ³/₄-inch squares, keeping beet colors separate to avoid color bleeding. Season each with oil, vinegar, salt, and pepper.

**To make the Beet Reduction:** Cut beets into ½-inch pieces and juice in a juicer, discarding solids. If no juicer is available, use a blender and blend with a little bit of water until smooth, straining solids through a fine mesh sieve. Put the beet juice into a small saucepan over low heat. Reduce juice by two-thirds, or until a syrup-like consistency. Strain the juice through a fine mesh sieve, chill, and set aside.

**To make the Walnut Chutney:** Place walnuts and olive oil in a large sauté pan over medium-low heat. Stir constantly until walnuts are light brown and evenly toasted, about 3 minutes. Immediately transfer nuts into another container to stop the cooking process. Once the nuts are cool, chop or pulse in a food processor until fine. Place chopped nuts in a medium-size bowl and mix with walnut oil, syrup, vinegar, mustard powder, salt, and pepper; set aside.

**To make the Croutons:** Preheat oven to 350 degrees F. Remove the crust from the bread. With a serrated knife, cut bread into slices about ⅛-inch thick. Cut slices into 2½ x ½-inch rectangles. Line a baking sheet with parchment paper, brush with half the oil and sprinkle with a very thin layer of salt and pepper. Place at least 30 bread rectangles in a single layer on top of the parchment paper. Brush another piece of parchment paper with remaining oil, sprinkle with salt and pepper, and then place on top of the bread, oil side down.

## CHIVE OIL
½ bunch chives
2 tablespoons olive oil

## GARNISH
1 cup baby arugula leaves
4 baby white turnips, very thinly sliced (preferably on a mandoline)
3 tablespoons freshly grated horseradish

Place another baking sheet of the same size on top to weigh down the bread pieces and prevent curling while baking. Bake for 6 minutes, or until golden brown and crisp; remove and set aside. Note that the yield might be greater than needed for one recipe.

To make the Chive Oil: Roughly chop chives and blend with oil on high until paste-like. Put the paste into a small sauté pan over medium-high heat. Allow the mixture to boil for about 30 seconds while stirring frequently. The paste will start to separate and release its chlorophyll, causing the oil to turn bright green. Once the bubbles start to subside, remove pan from heat, strain immediately through a fine mesh sieve, and refrigerate. Be careful not to cook too long or the oil will turn brown and the solids will fry.

How to Plate: Boil about 2 cups water with 1 teaspoon salt. Cook turnip slices in boiling water for 10 seconds and then shock in ice water. Cool and then strain; set aside.

Brush a straight line of Beet Reduction down the center of six chilled rectangular plates. (Important to chill the plates for the beet reduction to adhere to them well.)

Place an even amount of Beet Salad around the reduction. Garnish each plate with baby arugula, thinly sliced turnip, 3 Croutons, 2 spoonfuls of Walnut Chutney, Chive Oil, and a sprinkling of fresh horseradish. Serve immediately.

# Zucchini Boxes Provençal with Black Mosto Oil, Red Pickled Shallots, and Opal Basil

SERVES 6

## ZUCCHINI BOXES

10 medium zucchini, washed
  and trimmed

1 tablespoon salt

4 plum tomatoes

1 large Spanish onion, diced

3 tablespoons olive oil

3 cloves garlic, peeled

2 sprigs thyme

Salt and ground white pepper to taste

To make the Zucchini Boxes: Using a vegetable slicer or a mandoline, cut zucchini lengthwise into at least 72 long, very thin rectangular slices that are about 1½ inches wide. Use only the external portion and not the seeded portion. Trim the rest of the zucchini around the seeds. Discard the seeds and cut the remainder of zucchini into a small dice and reserve for stuffing.

Bring a large pot of water to a boil and add salt. Set a bowl of ice water to the side. Cook the sliced zucchini in the boiling water for about 30 seconds and then remove and place in the ice water. Remove from the ice water, pat dry, and set aside. Reserve the boiling water and the ice water.

Score the bottom of each plum tomato and remove the core with a small paring knife. Place the tomatoes in the boiling water. Cook for about 5 to 10 seconds, then remove with a slotted spoon and shock in the ice water. Remove from the water when chilled and peel with a small paring knife, pulling the skin from the scored bottom to the top. Cut the tomatoes in half lengthwise and scoop out the seeds, reserving for garnish. Cut the tomatoes into small dice.

In a large sauté pan over medium heat, sauté the onion with the oil, garlic, and thyme for about 1 minute. Add the diced zucchini and continue to cook until the onions are translucent and the zucchini is tender. Add the tomato, salt, and pepper, and cook until most of the water is evaporated. Remove from the heat and chill.

Line a 2-inch-square mold (1 inch high) with 4 zucchini slices (2 horizontal and 2 vertical) allowing the edges to hang over the mold. Stuff three-fourths full with the vegetable mixture. Fold the overhanging zucchini on top of the vegetables, trimming if necessary with scissors. Press lightly on the vegetables to make sure they are tightly packed.

*Recipe continued on next page*

## BLACK MOSTO OIL

1 cup dry-cured Moroccan black olives

⅓ cup olive oil

½ tablespoon Tabasco

1 tablespoon balsamic vinegar

Salt and pepper to taste

## PICKLED SHALLOTS

3 whole shallots

¼ cup distilled vinegar

¼ cup red wine vinegar

1 tablespoon grenadine

1 tablespoon sugar

## GARNISH

Fleur de sel

½ cup extra virgin olive oil

½ cup plum tomato seeds (reserved
   from plum tomatoes)

⅓ cup small opal basil leaves

2 tablespoons picked thyme leaves

Turn the mold over onto a baking sheet lined with oiled parchment paper and remove the mold carefully, keeping the square shape of the box. Repeat this process to make 18 boxes. Brush each box with oil and sprinkle with thyme leaves and freshly ground white pepper.

Preheat oven to 275 degrees F. Bake for 10 to 12 minutes. The boxes should be served warm, not hot.

To make the Black Mosto Oil: Preheat oven to 200 degrees F. Smash the olives with a flat object or the palm of your hand and remove the pits. Put the olives on a baking sheet and bake for about 2 hours, or until the olives feel very dry.

Put the dried olives in a blender and add the oil. Blend on high speed until a smooth liquid is formed. Add Tabasco, vinegar, salt, and pepper. Chill and set aside.

To make the Pickled Shallots: Remove the skin from the shallots with a sharp paring knife. Slice the shallots horizontally to make thin rings.

In a medium saucepot, bring the vinegars, grenadine, and sugar to a boil. Add the shallots and return to a boil, remove from the heat, and cool.

How to Plate: Place 3 warm Zucchini Boxes on each of six square plates, seasoning the top with fleur de sel. Artfully garnish each plate with dots of oil, plum tomato seeds, and opal basil leaves. Using a teaspoon of Black Mosto Oil, slide and gently pour between the boxes to create two narrow lines across the plate. Top each box with 2 pickled shallots and thyme.

# Spiced Citrus Fruit Salad with Pineapple Sorbet, Toasted Nut Tuile, and Pineapple Chip

SERVES 10

## MEYER LEMON CONFIT

5 Meyer lemons (or regular lemons
   can be substituted)
3 cups water
4 cups granulated sugar, divided
¾ cup light corn syrup

To make the Meyer Lemon Confit: Bring three large pots of water to a boil. Cut lemons in half, squeeze, and reserve juice. Boil lemons for 1 minute; drain and rinse. Repeat in second pot. Put lemons in third pot and simmer until tender (you can check with the tip of a paring knife); chill. With a spoon, scrape away the pith, which should be very soft and easy to remove. In a medium saucepan, bring 3 cups of water to a boil with 3 cups sugar. Add the lemon skins and bring to a simmer. Remove from heat and cover. Store at room temperature for up to 2 days. Reheat with remaining sugar and light corn syrup until sugar is dissolved. Store, covered, in refrigerator until ready to use. Slice the skins into three petals each.

*Recipe continued on next page*

## PINEAPPLE SORBET

1¼ cups water

¾ cup sugar

¼ cup corn syrup

½ teaspoon scraped vanilla bean

1¾ cups pineapple purée

## FRUIT SOUP

1 cup orange juice

⅓ cup water

1 ounce or 2-inch knob fresh ginger,
  peeled and roughly chopped

1 vanilla bean, sliced down the
  middle horizontally

10 star anise

1 tablespoon apple pectin (optional)

½ cup sugar

## TOASTED NUT TUILE

⅓ cup macadamia nuts, cut into
  quarters

¼ cup pine nuts

1 cup sugar

⅓ cup water

¼ teaspoon cream of tartar

¼ cup finely ground pistachios

## PINEAPPLE CHIPS

½ pineapple (reserved from
  Fruit Salad)

¼ cup powdered sugar

To make the Pineapple Sorbet: Combine the water, sugar, and corn syrup in a large saucepan over high heat and bring to a boil. When the sugar is dissolved, whisk in vanilla bean and pineapple purée; remove from the heat. Using a hand blender or standing blender, purée the mix well. Chill overnight in the refrigerator. The next day, put the mix into an ice cream maker and spin until semi-solid. Store in the freezer.

To make the Fruit Soup: Combine the orange juice, water, ginger, vanilla bean, and star anise in a medium-size saucepan and bring to a boil. Remove from the heat and let sit at room temperature for about 45 minutes. Strain through a fine mesh sieve and return to the saucepan. Combine the apple pectin (if using) and sugar, then whisk into the soup. Return to the heat and simmer, whisking, for 1 minute. Remove the pot from the heat, transfer the soup to another container and chill.

To make the Toasted Nut Tuile: Preheat oven to 300 degrees F. Toast the macadamia nuts and pine nuts on a baking sheet in the oven for about 3 to 4 minutes, or until golden brown; cool. Increase oven temperature to 320 degrees F. In a small saucepan over high heat, combine the sugar, water, and cream of tartar. Checking the mixture with a candy thermometer, bring the mixture up to 329 degrees F (165 degrees C). Remove from the heat, pour onto a baking sheet lined with a Silpat, and cool completely. When the mixture is completely hardened, break into chunks and blend in a food processor until it turns to a fine powder. Sprinkle the powder in one even layer with a small sieve into 1 x 3-inch rectangular molds on a baking sheet lined with Silpat. Bake for 5 to 8 minutes, or until the powder melts into a clear liquid. Remove from the oven and while still hot, place two macadamia nuts, three pine nuts, and a sprinkling of ground pistachio on top of each tuile; cool and set aside.

To make the Pineapple Chips: Preheat oven to 210 degrees F. Slice the pineapple paper-thin laterally using a professional slicing machine. (If you do not have access to one, you can use a very sharp serrated knife, making slices as thin as possible.) Using a sugar sifter, sprinkle a thin layer of powdered sugar on top of a nonstick

## FRUIT SALAD

6 mandarin oranges

5 blood oranges (or navel oranges can be substituted)

2 grapefruit

1 pineapple (half reserved for Pineapple Chips)

baking sheet, or on a regular baking sheet sprayed with nonstick spray; arrange the pineapple slices in one layer. Sprinkle lightly with powdered sugar. Place another nonstick baking sheet on top, or another regular baking sheet that has been lightly sprayed with nonstick spray on the bottom. (This will prevent the pineapple chips from curling during baking.) Bake 2½ hours, or until the chips are completely dry and crispy.

To make the Fruit Salad: Using a sharp paring knife, slice away and discard the peel of the mandarin oranges, blood oranges, and grapefruit, leaving only the flesh of the fruit and no white pith. Cut the citrus fruit into segments by slicing inward toward the center of the fruit on both sides of each segment; set aside. Cut the skin from the pineapple using a long serrated knife, first cutting off the top and bottom, and then slicing down the sides, following the shape of the pineapple, being careful not to remove too much of the flesh. Cut the pineapple in half widthwise and set aside one-half to make the Pineapple Chips. Cut the other half of the pineapple into ¼-inch dice, being careful not to use the core; set aside.

How to Plate: Chill ten bowls. On the bottom of each bowl, arrange three pieces of Meyer Lemon Confit in a flower-like pattern. Using a 1 x 3-inch rectangular mold, divide the pineapple dice evenly into each bowl. Remove the mold and arrange the citrus fruit segments in a straight line on top. Place one Toasted Nut Tuile flat on top of the citrus fruit. Spoon about ⅓ cup Fruit Soup around fruit in the bottom of each bowl. On top of the tuile, spoon 1 scoop Pineapple Sorbet. Place 1 Pineapple Chip in the middle of the sorbet, standing it straight up. Serve immediately.

NOTE: This recipe will take overnight steps.

# David Burke

*"Creating vegetable dishes? Love it! It is the way of the future and a nice challenge. It also gives us a chance to show off."*

David Burke's radical and whimsical approach to food and his artful presentations have made him a leading force in American cooking today. His fascination with vibrant ingredients and his unbridled creativity has fueled a brilliant career as a chef, artist, and entrepreneur as he has introduced revolutionary food products and cooking techniques.

A New Jersey native and graduate of the Culinary Institute of America, Burke refined his culinary skills in the kitchens of notable French chefs Pierre Trosgols, Georges Blanc, and Gaston Lenotre. At age 26 he became the first American and one of the youngest chefs in record to win France's coveted Meilleurs Ouvriers de France Diplome d'Honneur. The awards continued as he received Japan's Nippon Award of Excellence, the Robert Mondavi Award of Excellence, a Beard nomination for Best Chef: New York, and CIA's August Escoffier Award.

After working at the legendary River Café, Burke opened Park Avenue Cafe in 1992 and for twelve years served as vice president of Culinary Development for the Smith & Wollensky Restaurant Group. In 2003, Burke teamed with restaurateur Donatella Arpais to open davidburke & donatella. He expanded his empire with David Burke at Bloomingdale's, Primehouse in Chicago's James Hotel, Fromagerie in Rumson, New Jersey, and the eye-popping David Burke Las Vagas in the Venetian Resort Hotel Casino. Burke is a board member of Research Chefs Association, an advisor for J. Manheimer, Inc., and the author of two cookbooks, *Cooking with David Burke* and *David Burke's New American Classics.*

# Yellow Gazpacho and Ratatouille

SERVES 6 TO 8

## GAZPACHO

1 tablespoon cumin seeds

1 tablespoon coriander seeds

1 tablespoon celery seeds

6 ripe yellow beefsteak tomatoes,
  roughly chopped

3 cucumbers, peeled, seeded, and
  roughly chopped

3 yellow peppers, cored, seeded and
  roughly chopped

2 red onions, roughly chopped

1 bunch cilantro, roughly chopped

1 jalapeño pepper, seeded and
  chopped

2 cups sherry vinegar

1 cup extra virgin olive oil

Tabasco, salt, and pepper to taste

## RATATOUILLE

1 tablespoon canola oil

1 red bell pepper, finely diced

1 yellow bell pepper, finely diced

1 eggplant, finely diced

1 yellow squash, finely diced

1 zucchini, finely diced

1 red onion, finely diced

3 cloves garlic, finely chopped

Salt and pepper to taste

$2/3$ cup prepared tomato sauce

$1/4$ cup finely chopped fresh basil

1 or 2 corn tortillas

## GARNISH

1 scallion, julienned

To make the Gazpacho: Toast the cumin, coriander, and celery seeds in a nonstick skillet until aromatic. Cool, and then grind in a spice grinder until fine. Combine all of the ingredients except Tabasco, salt, and pepper in a bowl and marinate overnight. Purée in a food processor and strain out pulp. Season with Tabasco, salt, and pepper; refrigerate.

To make the Ratatouille: Heat oil in a 10-inch sauté pan. In small batches, sauté vegetables until slightly brown and crispy. Remove and place into a mixing bowl. Season with garlic, salt, and pepper to taste. Bind with tomato sauce and basil.

Heat oven to 350 degrees F. Cut the corn tortilla into $1/4$-inch strips. Place on a baking sheet and top with another. Crisp for about 10 minutes; cool.

How to Plate: Fill a large wine glass about one-third to one-half full (depending on the size of the glass) with Gazpacho and float a teaspoon of Ratatouille in the center with the scallion julienne.

Place a $1^1/2$ x 3-inch-ring mold in the center of a side plate. Carefully fill mold with Ratatouille and pack to remove any excess liquid. Let set momentarily, then carefully slide a turner underneath and transport to a dinner plate; remove mold. Add two corn tortilla strips as garnish. Serve immediately.

# Vegetable Carousel Torte with Pomme Soufflés filled with Peas

MAKES 4 ENTREES, DEPENDING UPON MOLDS USED

## VEGETABLE TORTE

1 cup broccoli florets, blanched and shocked

1 cup cauliflower florets, blanched and shocked

2 zucchini, sliced on the bias ¼ inch

2 squash, sliced on the bias ¼ inch

Extra virgin olive oil

Salt and pepper to taste

2 large leeks, well cleaned and diced (white parts only)

2 red peppers, roasted and sliced

1 cup spinach, stems removed, blanched and shocked

## MASHED POTATOES

4 large potatoes, peeled and boiled

Olive oil

Salt and pepper to taste

## BASIL OIL

3 cups basil, blanched and shocked

3 cups extra virgin olive oil

## POMME SOUFFLÉ

2 potatoes, peeled, shaped into an oval, and sliced on a mandoline

2 pots canola oil, 3 inches deep, one at 300 degrees F and the other at 400 degrees F

12 ounces garden peas, blanched and reserved warm (frozen can be substituted)

To make the Vegetable Torte: Set aside the blanched and shocked broccoli and cauliflower florets. Toss zucchini and squash with oil until well-coated and then season with salt and pepper. Grill on each side for 1 minute, do not mark; reserve warm. Sweat leeks in a little oil until tender and purée in a blender with about 2 tablespoons oil until smooth; reserve.

To make the Mashed Potatoes: Rice potatoes, or hand beat, or use low-speed setting on a mixer. Add oil until creamy. Season with salt and pepper; reserve warm.

To make the Basil Oil: Squeeze excess water from basil. Purée in a blender with oil until warm to the touch. Strain through double layers of cheesecloth and reserve for plating.

NOTE: This will make more than needed for this recipe and can be used for other meals as a substitute for butter, pasta dishes, and seasoning for vegetables.

To make the Pomme Soufflé: Slice potatoes $1/8$- to $1/4$-inch thick on a Japanese mandoline. Rest in ice water for 30 minutes. Remove from water and with extreme care place potato slices in a pot of oil at 300 degrees F. Shake constantly and fry for 6 to 7 minutes. They should rise to the top after 5 minutes. (The ice-cold potatoes added to the hot oil will cause the potatoes to steam, brown, and soufflé.) Place the potatoes into a pot of oil at 400 degrees F to crisp. They will puff up; continue to fry until golden brown. Be extremely careful as the hot oil will spit; drain. Serve, stuffed with peas as soon as torte is unmolded.

To assemble Torte: Grease a 2¹/₂ x 4-inch mold lightly with oil. Place on the dinner plate. For the base, press 3 zucchini slices and 3 squash slices into the mold with back of a spoon or a spatula. Follow with broccoli and cauliflower florets, followed by red pepper slices. Press ¹/₄ cup spinach on top of peppers. Spoon leek purée over top. Fill mold to the top with Mashed Potatoes and flatten with a spatula. Bake in a 425-degree F oven for 10 minutes.

How to Plate: Carefully unmold Vegetable Torte onto a plate. Drizzle Basil Oil around the base and top with 3 Pomme Soufflés filled with garden peas. To save a step, skip making the Pomme Souffles and simply line a row of nicely spaced peas around the top edge of the mashed potatoes. Serve immediately.

# Sweet Pea Ravioli with Sautéed Pea Leaves

SERVES 6 AS AN APPETIZER OR 4 AS AN ENTRÉE (YIELDS 20 RAVIOLI)

## RAVIOLI DOUGH

1 pound all-purpose flour

3 tablespoons tapioca starch

1 cup water

6 tablespoons olive oil

## RAVIOLI FILLING

3 shallots, minced

3 cups English peas, blanched

4 ounces soft tofu

½ cup extra virgin olive oil

Salt and pepper to taste

## PEA CREAM

1 bunch asparagus

3 ounces soft tofu

4 bunches baby spinach, cleaned

2 cups English peas, blanched

## CHILI OIL

1 shallot, minced

2 cloves garlic, minced

1 teaspoon cayenne pepper

1 teaspoon paprika

1 teaspoon chili powder

1 teaspoon red pepper flakes

1½ teaspoons chopped green onion

1 tablespoon fresh oregano

1 tablespoon dried oregano

½ tablespoon coarse or kosher salt

1½ cups olive oil

To make the Ravioli Dough: Mix the dough ingredients together to form a smooth dough. Wrap in plastic and refrigerate for 1 hour.

To make the Ravioli Filling: Sweat shallots in a light covering of oil in a heavy-bottomed saucepan until soft and translucent. Add peas and tofu and slowly heat. Purée in a food processor with oil until smooth. Season with salt and pepper.

To assemble the Ravioli: Roll out Ravioli Dough on a flour-coated surface until paper-thin. Cut into 1-inch strips. Spoon 1 tablespoon filling onto strips of dough at 1 inch intervals. Moisten edges with oil and lay strips of dough on top of filling. Press lightly around each filling mound to seal and then cut into squares.

To make the Pea Cream: Cut asparagus into 1-inch lengths, place in a saucepan, and cover with water. Slowly bring to a simmer. Add tofu and spinach leaves along with the peas for about 3 minutes. Purée, strain, and set aside.

To make the Chili Oil: Combine all ingredients in a heavy-bottomed saucepan. Simmer over very low heat for about 10 minutes, or until flavors are extracted from ingredients. Be careful not to let spices brown. The chili flavor will be enjoyed in a subtle taste suspended in the oil.

## GARNISH

2 shallots, minced

1 cup English peas

½ pound pea tendrils and popcorn
shoots (available in the summer)

How to Plate: Poach ravioli for 4 minutes, or until cooked; drain. In a large skillet, sauté shallots in a small amount of oil and add peas. Add Pea Cream slowly and bring to a simmer. Add ravioli and season with salt and pepper. Pour carefully into a shallow bowl. Garnish with Chili Oil and peas and shallots. Garnish with summer pea tendrils and popcorn shoots or other favorite decorative greens. Serve immediately.

# Stir-Fried Fruit and Peach Sorbet

SERVES 8 TO 10

*Heidi Kohnhorstf, Pastry Chef*

4 tablespoons blended oil (90 percent
   vegetable/10 percent olive)

¼ teaspoon salt

1 small piece gingerroot, peeled,
   boiled, and julienned

1 stalk lemongrass, smashed
   and minced (lemon zest can
   be substituted)

½ pineapple, cored and cut

2 mangoes, peeled and diced

2 peaches, sliced in wedges

½ cup sugar

4 star fruit, sliced

4 kiwi, peeled and sliced

Peach sorbet, purchased

Heat a sauté pan and add oil, salt, gingerroot, and lemongrass. Cook a few minutes. Add the pineapple, mangoes, and peaches and cook until juices pull out. Add sugar and star fruit. Cook a little longer, turn off heat, and gently add the kiwi. Serve at room temperature with a scoop of peach sorbet.

# Eric Ripert

*"Following a vegan diet doesn't have to be boring if you cook with talent and heart—you'll have great and exciting dishes in front of you to enjoy."*

Eric Ripert's early passion for food was fueled in large part by his family and early exposure to the cuisines of Antibes and Andorra. At fifteen he left home to attend culinary school in Perpignan, and two years later, he moved to Paris to cook at the legendary La Tour D'Argent and at Jamin. After military service, Ripert returned to Jamin to work with celebrated chef Joel Robuchon. In 1989, Ripert moved to Washington, D.C., to be sous chef for Jean-Louis Palladin at Watergate. In 1991, he relocated to New York, working briefly for David Bouley before becoming chef at Le Bernadin.

At only twenty-nine years old, Ripert earned his first four-star review from the *New York Times*. His second four-star review earned Le Bernardin its unique standing as the only New York venue ever to sustain four consecutive four-star reviews over an extended period of time. *GQ* has named Le Bernardin the best restaurant in America, and it has garnered three stars from Zagat for Best Food in New York City for six consecutive years. James Beard Foundation awarded Ripert and the restaurant top honors for Outstanding Restaurant of the Year (1998), Outstanding Service (1999), Top Chef: New York City (1999), and Outstanding Chef in the United States (2003). Since 2006, he's earned the coveted three-stars for Le Bernadin from the Michelin Guide and has opened restaurants for the Ritz-Carlton, Grand Cayman, and in Washington, D.C. As chair of City Harvest's Food Council, he has helped raise money and the quality of food donations through working with other top chefs and restaurants. He has authored two cookbooks—*A Return to Cooking* and *Le Bernardin Cookbook* with coauthor Maguy Le Coze.

# Snow Morels with a Medley of Spring Beans and Peas and Yuzu Vinaigrette

SERVES 4

## YUZU VINAIGRETTE

1 tablespoon white miso paste

1 tablespoon yuzu juice (lime juice
can be substituted)

¼ cup canola oil

Fine sea salt and freshly ground
pepper to taste

## SNOW MORELS, SPRING BEANS, AND PEAS

1 teaspoon olive oil

2 teaspoons minced shallot

1 teaspoon minced garlic

20 large snow morels, cleaned

Fine sea salt and freshly ground
pepper to taste

2 tablespoons fava beans, shelled,
blanched, skinned, and split in half

2 tablespoons baby peas, shelled,
blanched, and split in half

8 sugar snap peas, cut into short
julienne

24 hon-shimeji mushrooms,
trimmed right below the cap
(about 2 ounces)

## GARNISH

2 tablespoons julienned daikon radish

2 tablespoons enoki mushrooms,
rinsed, cut 1-inch from the tip

½ cup Affillia cress (similar to micro
pea shoots) or use another mild
microgreen

To make the Yuzu Vinaigrette: Combine miso paste and yuzu in a small bowl; whisk until frothy. Continue to whisk and slowly drizzle in oil. Season with salt and pepper; set aside.

To make the Snow Morels, Spring Beans, and Peas: Heat oil in a small pan. Sweat shallot and garlic in oil until soft, about 2 minutes. Add snow morels and sauté over low heat for a few minutes until tender and most of the liquid has evaporated. Season with salt and pepper. Add beans, baby peas, sugar snap peas, and hon-shimeji mushrooms; toss to warm without getting color and season to taste.

How to Plate: Arrange 5 snow morels in a line on the center of each plate, leaving some space between each. Garnish the morels with beans, baby peas, and sugar snap peas. Arrange six hon-shimeji mushrooms around the morels. Sprinkle the daikon radish and enoki mushrooms over the morels. Arrange a layer of Affillia cress over the morels. Drizzle 1 tablespoon Yuzu Vinaigrette around the plate.

# Grilled Eggplant, Stuffed Sweet Pepper, and Marinated Zucchini and Celery with Tandoori Tomato Sauce

SERVES 4

## TANDOORI TOMATO SAUCE

2 tablespoons sliced shallot

1 tablespoon sliced garlic

1 tablespoon olive oil

2 tomatoes, peeled, seeded, and chopped

½ tablespoon Sharwood's tandoori powder or Tandoori Masala

Fine sea salt and freshly ground pepper

## GRILLED EGGPLANT, STUFFED SWEET PEPPER, AND MARINATED ZUCCHINI AND CELERY

1 large eggplant

2 tablespoons hummus

1 tablespoon fresh lemon juice

Fine sea salt and freshly ground pepper to taste

4 yellow baby peppers, roasted, peeled and seeds carefully removed, keeping peppers whole

¼ cup extra virgin olive oil

To make the Tandoori Tomato Sauce: Sweat shallot and garlic in oil until tender, about 3 to 4 minutes. Add tomatoes and tandoori; season with salt and pepper. Cook for 15 to 20 minutes, or until tomatoes fall apart and flavors come together. Press through a chinois until pulp comes through and sauce is thick; set aside.

To make the Grilled Eggplant, Stuffed Sweet Pepper, and Marinated Zucchini and Celery: Preheat oven to 375 degrees F. Cut eggplant in half crosswise and reserve the thicker part. Cut thinner part in half lengthwise. Place eggplant in a lightly oiled pan, cut-side down, with just enough water to go ¼-inch up the side of the pan. Cover the pan with aluminum foil and roast the eggplant until tender, about 30 minutes. Remove eggplant from oven and cool slightly. When cool enough to handle, scoop out the flesh and put ½ cup in a small food processor. Add the hummus and lemon juice; purée until smooth and season with salt and pepper. Fill the peppers with the stuffing, slightly folding in the ends of each pepper; reserve.

Preheat a grill or grill pan. Peel the remaining eggplant. Cut four 3 x 3-inch squares that are ¼ inch thick from the eggplant. Marinate with salt, pepper and oil. Grill eggplant on both sides until tender. Place the stuffed peppers on the grill to heat them as well without getting color. Gently warm the Tandoori Tomato Sauce.

## GARNISH

1 teaspoon fresh lemon juice

2 teaspoons extra virgin olive oil

Salt and freshly ground pepper to taste

1 zucchini, including green peel, cut
into 12 (4 x ¼ x ¼-inch) strips

2 stalks celery, cut into 12 (4 x
¼ x ¼-inch) strips

How to Plate: Make a lemon vinaigrette by whisking together the lemon juice and oil. Season with salt and pepper. Toss the zucchini and celery with the lemon vinaigrette. Drape 3 zucchini and 3 celery strips over each stuffed pepper. Drizzle Tandoori Tomato Sauce around the eggplant. Serve warm.

# Apple Confit, Quince Ras el Hanout Purée, Poached Dates, and Apple Chips

### SERVES 4

*Michael Laiskonis, Pastry Chef (James Beard 2007 Outstanding Pastry Chef in U.S.)*

## CINNAMON CARAMEL POWDER

½ cup granulated sugar
⅛ cup water
¾ teaspoon ground cinnamon
½ vanilla bean, split and scraped

## APPLE CONFIT

4 pounds Granny Smith apples, peeled
   and cored

## APPLE SORBET

4 pounds Granny Smith apples,
   peeled, cored, and chopped
½ cup water
¾ cup granulated sugar

## POACHED DATES

8 whole dates, pitted
½ cup water
¼ cup granulated sugar
1 lemon, juiced

**To make the Cinnamon Caramel Powder:** Combine sugar and water in a small pot. Without stirring, cook mixture over medium heat until all the sugar has dissolved and the mixture turns a medium amber color. Remove the caramel from the heat and stir in cinnamon and vanilla bean scrapings. Pour the caramel onto a Silpat on a baking sheet. Place a second Silpat on top of the caramel and flatten carefully with a rolling pin. Allow the caramel to cool and set at room temperature. When set, pulverize the dried caramel in a coffee bean grinder into a fine powder. Store in an airtight container until ready to use.

**To make the Apple Confit:** Preheat oven to 325 degrees F. Slice apples crosswise as thinly as possible. Lightly grease half of a 5 x 9 x 3-inch-deep baking pan or glass baking dish with nonstick spray. Sprinkle 1 tablespoon Cinnamon Caramel Powder in the bottom of the pan. Arrange one layer of apple slices on top, slightly overlapping. Sprinkle 2 tablespoons Cinnamon Caramel Powder over the apple slices; repeat layers. Cover the pan with aluminum foil and bake until tender, about 45 to 60 minutes. Remove the foil and place a sheet of parchment paper cut to fit the pan on top of the apples. Place a second pan or dish on top of the apples, gently pressing them down to cool for at least 2 hours. Cover tightly with plastic wrap and refrigerate until ready to serve.

**To make the Apple Sorbet:** Place apples and water in a medium saucepan and cook covered over low heat until softened. Add sugar and purée until smooth. Force through a fine-mesh sieve to ensure removal of any bits of seed or core. Cool then process in an ice cream maker according to the manufacturer's directions.

**To make the Poached Dates:** Soak dates in cold water for at 1 hour. Peel skin from dates. Combine water, sugar, and lemon juice in a saucepan and bring to a boil. Add dates and reduce heat to low, poaching for 5 minutes; cool.

### APPLE GELEE

1 cup apple cider
1 tablespoon granulated sugar
½ teaspoon agar-agar powder

### QUINCE RAS EL HANOUT PURÉE

1 small quince (if out of season, use
    an apple)
1½ cups water
¾ cup granulated sugar
1 tablespoon ras el hanout*

*Ras el hanout is an aromatic North
African spice blend, literally translated
as "top of the market." It is often
composed of a dozen or more spices
and flowers. If unavailable, substitute
cinnamon sticks, clove, cardamom,
black pepper, rosehips, or star anise.

### APPLE CHIPS

1 Granny Smith apple
½ cup sugar
½ cup water
½ cup pineapple juice

To make the Apple Gelee: Combine all ingredients in a small saucepan. Gently bring to a boil, reduce heat, and simmer for 2 minutes. Remove from heat and let stand. Meanwhile, place a sheet of plastic wrap onto a baking sheet. Pour mixture onto the baking sheet so gelee will spread and set. Chill and cut into squares to drape over the Poached Dates.

To make the Quince Ras El Hanout Purée: Peel, core, and roughly chop the quince. Combine with remaining ingredients in a saucepan and cook over low heat until tender. Remove any pieces of spices and purée mixture, adding a little water if necessary to make sauce smooth.

To make the Apple Chips: Preheat oven to 200 degrees F. Peel half of the apple and slice as thinly as possible (you need four good slices). Place apple slices in a shallow dish. Make simple syrup by heating the sugar and water together in a small pot. Once the sugar has dissolved, add the pineapple juice and return syrup to a boil. Pour syrup over apple slices; poach for 5 minutes, then remove apple slices and drain. Arrange apple slices flat and not touching on a Silpat on a baking sheet. Dry apple slices in a 200-degree F oven until crisp, about 1 hour. Store chips in an airtight container until ready to serve.

How to Plate: Cut eight 2-inch circles from the Apple Confit with a round metal cutter and place two circles on each plate. Arrange the Poached Dates and Apple Gelee along one side of the confit and place a scoop of the Apple Sorbet on the other. Finish with the Quince Ras el Hanout Purée and Apple Chip. Serve immediately.

# Erik Blauberg

*"It is so important that all chefs take the dietary needs of their customers seriously. Vegan dishes have been in demand a long time, and no longer will a plate of vegetables do. All diners should expect to have a dish as exciting as all the other items on the menu."*

Erik Blauberg's fascination with food began at an early age when he would sneak into hotel kitchens in the Catskills and watch chefs at work. From his humble culinary beginnings flipping burgers, he traveled to the French kitchens of Paul Bocuse and Roger Verge and the Imperial Hotel in Tokyo and Kicho in Osaka. In New York, he sharpened his culinary skills at Bouley, La Cote Basque, Windows on the World, Tavern on the Green, and American Renaissance. After a stint at the five-star Jalousie Plantation Caribbean Resort and rave reviews from the *New York Times* and *New York Magazine* at Colors in New York, in 1996 Blauberg was recruited to be master chef at the world-renowned 21 Club in New York.

Blauberg is a culinary historian, an avid traveler, a truffle hunter, and an accomplished food photographer. He has been named One of the World's Great Chefs in the Culinary Institute of America's Great Chef Series, served as executive chef for the twelfth annual James Beard Holiday Auction, and was a Master Chef for a celebrated all-truffle dinner at the James Beard House with Charlie Trotter, David Bouley, and Jean Louis Palladin. He has been named One of the World's Best Chefs by the Academy of Hospitality Sciences and received the Five-Diamond Award, and a special achievement Jay Walman award. He serves on the advisory board of Syracuse University and frequently appears on the Food Network, at charity events, and on television in Japan, Germany, and England. He is currently the owner and CEO of EKB Restaurant Consulting and is responsible for overhauling the food programs for several large venues in New York City.

# Baby Frisée with Organic Wheat Berries, Winter Truffles, and Mustard Emulsion

SERVES 4

## WHEAT BERRIES

2 tablespoons soy margarine or
   olive oil

¼ cup finely minced onion

¼ cup finely minced celery

¼ cup finely minced carrots

½ cup organic wheat berries

Sea salt to taste

1 cup vegetable stock or water, divided

White pepper, freshly ground

## TRUFFLE MUSTARD EMULSION

Juice of 1 lemon, strained

3 tablespoons Dijon mustard

½ cup (4 ounces) truffle oil

Sea salt and freshly ground white
   pepper to taste

1 tablespoon minced truffles

## FRISÉE AND TRUFFLES

3 ounces baby frisée, center leaves
   picked, washed, and cut into
   small pieces

Salt and pepper to taste

1 large winter or summer truffle: thinly
   slice half, fine julienne other half

To make the Wheat Berries: In a saucepan over medium heat, melt soy margarine. Add and sauté onion, celery, and carrots until softened. Add wheat berries and stir. Season with sea salt and cook for 5 minutes. Add ½ cup vegetable stock, bring to a simmer, and reduce heat to low. Once the stock is absorbed, add the remaining ½ cup and continue to simmer until completely absorbed.

NOTE: More stock might be needed if the wheat berries remain too firm. Adjust seasoning with salt and pepper to taste. Cool and reserve.

To make the Truffle Mustard Emulsion: In a wooden bowl, whisk lemon juice and mustard until smooth. Slowly stream in truffle oil, whisking vigorously. Season with salt and pepper. Add the minced truffles. Whisk again just before serving.

To make the Frisée and Truffles: Place the baby frisée into a mixing bowl, lightly dress with the Truffle Mustard Emulsion, season with salt and pepper, and then toss. Add truffle julienne.

How to Plate: Pack Wheat Berries into a triangular mold and place in the center of a chilled plate; or spoon onto the center of the plate, pressing into a desired shape.

Gently place the Frisée and Truffles on top of the Wheat Berries. Drizzle the Truffle Mustard Emulsion around the plate. Garnish the frisée with the sliced truffles and serve immediately.

# Brûlée of Vermicelli Pasta with Lobster, Matsutake, and Blue Foot Mushrooms, and Tomato Marjoram Bouillon

SERVES 4

## BRÛLÉE OF VERMICELLI PASTA

1½ quarts corn oil

1 pound vermicelli

Salt

## MUSHROOMS

3 tablespoons olive oil

2½ cups mixed wild mushrooms
   (lobster, matsutake, blue foot,
   enoki), cleaned and sliced

2 tablespoons finely minced shallots

2 tablespoons tomato concassé
   (see note)

1 tablespoon margarine

2 tablespoons fresh marjoram leaves

Salt and pepper to taste

## TOMATO BOUILLON

2 cups fresh tomato juice (whole
   tomatoes cored and processed in
   a blender with a pinch of salt until
   liquefied, then strained through
   a cheesecloth)

1 tablespoon chopped fresh marjoram

½ tablespoon chopped lemongrass

Salt and pepper to taste

## GARNISH

Whole marjoram leaves

4 small bunches baby snow
   pea sprouts

To make the Brûlée of Vermicelli Pasta: Place the oil into a large saucepot and heat to about 325 degrees F. Carefully place the pasta into the oil and stir until golden brown. Turn off the heat and carefully remove pasta from oil; blot off any excess oil on a paper towel. Place the pasta into salted boiling water and cook until al dente, about 9 to 10 minutes depending on the pasta.

To make the Mushrooms: Place the oil in a hot sauté pan over medium heat. When it starts to lightly smoke, add the lobster mushrooms; toss and cook for 1 minute. Add the matsutake, and blue foot mushrooms and shallots, and continue to cook for 2 minutes. Add the enoki mushrooms, tomato concassé, margarine, and marjoram. Season with salt and pepper, remove from the pan, and reserve.

NOTE: To make tomato concassé, chose Roma tomatoes that are not too ripe. Score an X in the skin at the base of each tomato and blanch in boiling water for about 10 seconds until the skin begins to loosen. Remove from hot water and plunge into a bowl of ice water. The skin should now come off easily; if it doesn't, plunge back into boiling water for a few more seconds. Cut the tomatoes in quarters, remove the core and seeds, and cut into dice of the desired size.

To make the Tomato Bouillon: Add the tomato juice to a saucepan with the marjoram and lemongrass. Bring to a boil, and continue to boil for 2 minutes. Season with salt and pepper and strain with a cheesecloth. Reserve, keeping it hot.

How to Plate: Toss the Brûlée of Vermicelli Pasta into the Tomato Bouillon. Using a cook's fork, twirl the pasta onto a fork and place in the center of a hot plate. Remove the fork so that the pasta stands up on the plate. Artfully arrange the Mushrooms around the pasta, garnish with marjoram leaves and pea sprouts. Serve immediately.

# Terrine of White and Green Asparagus with Truffles and Beet Horseradish Dressing

SERVES 8

## WHITE ASPARAGUS PURÉE

6 tablespoons agar-agar

1 onion, minced

2 tablespoons olive oil

Sea salt and white pepper to taste

2 bunches white asparagus

1 cup asparagus stock, made by
　　reducing cooking water

1 teaspoon finely minced tarragon
　　leaves

## ASPARAGUS AND TRUFFLES

2 bunches green asparagus, standard
　　size, bottoms cut to fit terrine

½ bunch white asparagus, standard
　　size, bottoms cut to fit terrine

1 teaspoon vegetable oil

Opal basil leaves, picked (enough
　　to line a small loaf pan)

1 ounce black truffles, thinly sliced

½ cup chopped chervil

To make the White Asparagus Purée: Place agar-agar and 1¼ cups water into a saucepan and bring to a boil, reduce heat, and simmer until agar-agar is dissolved; set aside.

Sauté onion over medium heat in the oil until tender and translucent. Season with sea salt and white pepper. Remove from the pan, drain and blot off excess oil, and reserve.

Place the asparagus into slightly salted boiling water to cover for about 9 minutes, or until tender. Reserving the cooking stock, remove asparagus, and place into an ice bath to cool. Boil the asparagus cooking liquid to a reduction of 1 cup and cool.

Transfer the reduction to a blender, add the onion, tarragon, and asparagus, and blend at medium speed until smooth. Strain through a chinois and then place in a saucepan. Add dissolved agar-agar, stirring to combine, place over medium-high heat, and bring to a boil. Remove from heat; let cool to almost room temperature. While the purée cools, prepare the rest of the terrine.

To make the Asparagus and Truffles: Bring 4 quarts water to a boil. Drop in 1 bunch green asparagus at a time and cook for about 3½ minutes, then place in salted ice water until chilled. Repeat with white asparagus, cooking for 6½ minutes; pat dry and reserve.

Brush a 1-quart terrine mold (or small loaf pan) lightly with vegetable oil. Line with plastic wrap and make sure there are no air bubbles. Dip each opal basil leaf in the White Asparagus Purée and line the terrine, covering completely, slightly overlapping the leaves. Cut the green asparagus in half (widthwise) and split the white asparagus lengthwise; reserve.

*Recipe continued on page 110*

BEET HORSERADISH DRESSING
8 large beets, cut into small pieces
4 quarts water
¾ tablespoon champagne vinegar
2 tablespoons prepared horseradish
¾ cup olive oil
Sea salt and freshly ground white
   pepper to taste

GARNISH
Marjoram leaves
Black truffle slices

Line up and layer the green asparagus in the terrine. When halfway done, line the mold with one layer of split white asparagus. Pour White Asparagus Purée to barely cover the white asparagus. At this point add one layer of the thinly sliced black truffles, and then top with a layer of the white asparagus. Continue to layer the green asparagus until the mold is full. Then pour in the remaining purée until mold is filled. Shake the mold and tap lightly to release the air bubbles. Cover top with the chervil and lightly pat. Cover with plastic wrap and refrigerate overnight.

To make the Beet Horseradish Dressing: Process the beets in a food processor until finely minced. Transfer to a large saucepan and add the water. Cover, bring to a boil over high heat, and then reduce the heat to medium; let simmer for 30 minutes and strain, reserving the juice. Return the juice to the pan and continue simmering to reduce to 1 cup, or to desired consistency.

In a blender, combine the beet juice, champagne vinegar, and horseradish. Blend for 30 seconds and slowly add the oil in an even stream until all of it is incorporated into the juice mixture. Season with salt and white pepper. Reserve until ready to use.

How to Plate: To remove the terrine from the mold, carefully turn it upside down to release it. Remove the plastic wrap and slice the terrine with an electric knife. Place 1 slice in the center of each plate. Artfully drizzle the Beet Horseradish Dressing around the plate. Garnish with fresh marjoram leaves and a few slices of truffle.

# Gratin of Berries with Tahitian Vanilla Bean and Dark Rum

SERVES 4

½ cup small strawberries, stemmed

½ cup red raspberries

½ cup blueberries

½ cup black cherries, pitted and
   cut in half

1 cup red currants

½ cup white cherries, pitted and
   cut in half

½ cup small blackberries

½ cup boysenberries

4 tablespoons granulated sugar

2 ounces Grand Marnier

2 ounces dark rum

4 Tahitian vanilla beans, split,
   seeds only

1 cup raw cashew nuts, soaked
   about 6 hours

½ cup water

2 tablespoons maple syrup

GARNISH

Mint sprigs

Gently rinse all the berries and then place in a stainless steel bowl. Add the sugar, Grand Marnier, rum, and vanilla bean seeds; mix lightly. Cover and refrigerate for 1½ hours.

For the topping, blend together the cashews, water, and maple syrup in a high-speed blender until smooth. Add more water if needed for consistency. Remove the mixed berries from the refrigerator and distribute into four oven-safe casserole dishes. Top the berries with cashew cream. Place the casseroles in the oven under the broiler until lightly browned. (An option to the cashew cream is to whip 3 cups cold soy milk with 2 tablespoons powdered sugar and use in the same way.) Garnish with mint and serve immediately.

# Floyd Cardoz

*"It all comes down to the spices. It's as true today as it was back in my parent's kitchen all those years ago. Once you get to know Indian spices, they'll spark your imagination the way they do mine."*

Mumbai-born Floyd Cardoz decided to become a chef after making a chicken curry for his father in his home kitchen. He attended culinary school in Bombay, and received a diploma in Hotel Restaurant Management and Administration from the Les Roches culinary school in Switzerland. After an apprenticeship at the Taj Mahal Intercontinental Hotel, he worked in bustling kitchens in India, Italy, and France before joining celebrated New York chef Gray Kunz at Lepinasse. Cardoz's highly sophisticated cuisine featuring Eastern spices caught the attention of Kunz and national food writers. In 1988, Cardoz joined New York restaurateur Danny Meyer and Union Square chef Michael Romano as chef-partner at Tabla.

Tabla reflects Cardoz's vision for a new American and Indian fusion cuisine. Named after an Indian drum, its menu blends exotic flavors, aromatic Indian spices, fresh seasonal ingredients from local markets and tandoori-fired breads. Cardoz has been featured in numerous national magazines and has received critical accolades from the *Daily News,* the *New York Times,* and The James Beard Foundation. His first cookbook, *One Spice, Two Spice: American Food, Indian Flavors,* with *Gourmet* magazine senior features editor Jane Daniels Lear, is a tribute to his unique visionary fusion cuisine, a different way of thinking about food and spices. He introduces the spices that are the "bedrock of Indian cooking" into the modern American home cooks repertoire.

# Artichoke Bhel Puri

SERVES 6

1 cup whole fingerling potatoes

1 cup diced green mango, peeled and
   cut into ¼-inch dice

1 cup diced mutsu (or crispin) apple,
   cored and cut into ¼-inch dice

½ cup diced red onion, peeled and
   cut into ¼-inch dice

¼ cup coarsely chopped roasted
   peanuts

3 tablespoons mint chutney

3 tablespoons tamarind chutney

¼ cup cilantro leaves

2 tablespoons olive oil

2 tablespoons lime juice

1 teaspoon chaat masala

1 tablespoon minced green
   chile pepper

Salt to taste

¼ cup lemon juice

12 baby artichokes, cleaned
   and sliced thinly on a mandolin

Oil for frying, about 2 quarts

## GARNISH

1 cup sev (small chickpea noodles,
   a snack at most Indian stores)

Chive blossoms

Boil the whole fingerling potatoes in salted water until fork tender. Remove from the water and allow to cool. Cut in half lengthwise (or quarter if they are wider) then slice thinly crosswise to obtain small half moon or quarter moon shapes.

In a large bowl combine potatoes, mango, apple, onion, peanuts, chutneys, cilantro, oil, lime juice, chaat masala, chili pepper, and salt; mix thoroughly and set aside.

Fill a bowl with water and add the lemon juice. Pull off the outer dark leaves from the baby artichokes until the light pale leaves appear. Using a small sharp knife, peel the dark green layer off the stem. Cut off 1 inch from the top of the artichoke. With the top of the artichoke facing down, cut into paper thin slices. A mandolin works well for this. Add to the lemon water.

In a frying pan, heat the oil to 350 degrees F. In batches, remove a few artichoke slices from the water at a time, dry them very well with paper towels, and then fry them until they begin to color. Place in a strainer to drain any excess oil while you work on the rest of the artichokes. Once all artichokes are fried, repeat the process, frying them again until golden brown. Artichokes will be very crispy. Blot with paper towels to remove excess oil. Add the fried artichokes to the large bowl with the mixed ingredients and toss gently.

How to Plate: Place the Artichoke Bhel Puri in the center of a large bowl, gently pressing into a mound. Sprinkle the sev evenly over the mound and plate. Garnish with chive blossoms.

# Fricassee of Morels and Fava Beans, and Coconut Taro Purée

SERVES 4 TO 6

## TARO PURÉE

1 tablespoon canola oil

1 tablespoon chopped ginger

1 teaspoon chopped garlic

3 cups taro root, peeled and cut
   into 1-inch chunks

2 cups vegetable stock

3 cups coconut milk

Salt and pepper to taste

## FRICASSEE OF MORELS AND FAVA BEANS

2 tablespoons canola oil

4 cups morels, cleaned and cut
   into halves or quarters

Salt to taste

2 tablespoons minced shallots

2 tablespoons peeled and
   minced ginger

1 tablespoon sliced chiles

4 tablespoons white port wine

1 cup blanched fresh fava beans
   (pre-blanched frozen may be used)

¾ cup vegetable stock

1 teaspoon black cumin (shahi jeera)

½ cup cilantro, picked and cut
   into ribbons

¼ cup minced chives

**To make the Taro Purée:** Heat a 3-quart heavy-bottomed stewpot over moderate heat. Add the oil, ginger, and garlic, and cook for 1 minute. Add the taro root and sauté for 2 minutes. Add the vegetable stock, coconut milk, salt, and pepper. Cook, uncovered, until tender; drain, reserving the liquid. Purée in a food processor with a little liquid, adding more until a smooth and thick consistency is achieved. Keep warm until ready to serve.

**To make the Fricasse of Morels and Fava Beans:** Heat a gallon-size heavy bottomed stewpot over moderate heat for 2 minutes. Add the oil. When the oil starts to shimmer, add the morels and reduce the heat to medium-low. Season with salt and cook, stirring constantly, for 3 to 5 minutes. Add the shallots, ginger, and chiles, and cook for an additional 2 to 3 minutes. Deglaze the pan by adding the wine and stir to scrape up the caramelized bits from the bottom of the pan. Add the fava beans, vegetable stock, and black cumin, simmering for 2 minutes more. Adjust seasoning to taste and stir in the cilantro and chives. There should be some liquid left in the pan.

**How to Plate:** Distribute the Taro Purée in the center of four to six bowls, based on the portion size desired. Spoon the Fricassee of Morels and Fava Beans around the purée with the broth.

# Upma Polenta, Fricassee of Roasted Asparagus and Spring Onions

SERVES 6

## POLENTA

4 tablespoons canola oil, divided

3 cups Indian semolina ("Suji")

6 cups vegetable stock

1 teaspoon mustard seeds

½ teaspoon cumin seeds

2 tablespoons minced shallots

1 tablespoon sliced chiles

2 tablespoons minced ginger

2 tablespoons thinly sliced kokum

¼ cup cilantro, chiffonade

2 tablespoons chopped chives

Salt and pepper

## FRICASSEE

4 tablespoons extra virgin olive
oil, divided

2 cups sliced spring onions or
scallions, cut on the bias

2 tablespoons minced shallots

2 tablespoons thinly sliced kokum

2 bunches pencil asparagus, cut
into 1½-inch pieces

2 cups sliced spring garlic, about
1 head (if unavailable, use leeks)

2 cups sugar snap peas (about
7 ounces), cut in half on the bias

2 tablespoons minced ginger

1 teaspoon sliced chiles

Cilantro, chiffonade

Chives, chopped

Salt and pepper to taste

Leafy greens to garnish

To make the Polenta: Heat a 3-quart heavy-bottomed stewpot over medium-high heat and add 2 tablespoons oil. Add the semolina to the pot and toast, stirring constantly, until the semolina is lightly colored, about 8 to 10 minutes. This can be done up to a day in advance.

Heat the stock and keep hot. Heat a 3-quart pan over medium heat, add remaining oil and heat until it shimmers, about 2 minutes. Add the mustard and cumin seeds, and cook for 1 to 2 minutes, or until the mustard seeds start to pop. Add the shallots, chiles, and ginger, and cook until the shallots are translucent. Add the semolina and toast for 1 minute. Add the kokum, herbs, and hot stock; bring to a boil and turn off the heat. Season with salt and pepper. Cover with a tight-fitting lid and let set for 15 minutes. Before serving, use a fork to separate the grains.

To make the Fricassee: Place a large nonstick sauté pan over moderate heat and add 2 tablespoons oil. Add the onions and shallots, and stir-fry until translucent; add the kokum and cook for 1 minute more. Remove from pan and set aside.

Place a large heavy-bottomed stewpot over moderate heat. Add the remaining oil and, when warm, add the asparagus and garlic, sautéing while stirring constantly for 4 minutes. Add the sugar snap peas, stir-fried mixture, ginger, and chiles. Continue to cook for 3 to 4 minutes, stirring constantly. Add cilantro and chives, season with salt and pepper, and mix well. Cover and let set for 2 minutes before serving.

How to Plate: Distribute the Polenta among six plates, arranging in a mound in the center of each plate, or use a ring mold to create a flattened disk shape. Artfully arrange the Fricassee around the polenta and top with leafy greens, if desired.

# Gabriel Kreuther

*"Vegetables are an essence of nature . . . and cooking them together should be an exercise of harmony and flavor extraction."*

Raised on his family's farm outside of Strasbourg, Gabriel Kreuther grew up surrounded by fresh local produce. A natural love of cooking was nurtured by his mother and an uncle who owned a nearby hotel and restaurant. A culinary prize and gastronomic tour of North Africa began Kruether's culinary journey. He worked in legendary kitchens in Washington, D.C., Germany, and France; at L'Ermitage de Bernard Ravel, a two-star Michelin restaurant, he refined his signature artisan French-cooking style using organic herbs and plants to bring out the inherent flavors in a dish.

In 1977, Kreuther arrived at La Caravelle in New York and then worked four years at Jean-Georges. In 2001, he was named executive chef of Atelier in the Ritz Carlton on Central Park, where his talents won him a Best New Chef in *Food & Wine* magazine and a Best New Restaurant nomination by the James Beard Foundation. He subsequently garnered three stars in the *New York Times* and received the American Academy of Hospitality Sciences' prestigious Five-Star Diamond award. Since becoming executive chef at The Modern with the Union Square Hospitality Group, The Modern has been named a Best New Restaurant in *Esquire* magazine, Top Rated Zagat Newcomer and Time Out Best New Restaurant, and acquired a Michelin star. In 2006, The Modern was awarded three stars in the *New York Times* and won Best New Restaurant and Outstanding Restaurant Design by the James Beard Foundation. Kreuther received two James Beard award nominations for Best Chef: New York in 2006–2007.

# Yukon Gold Potato "Linguine" and Fresh Sprouts Salad with a Sorrel-Arugula Emulsion

SERVES 4

## SORREL-ARUGULA EMULSION

6 ounces sorrel (3 cups, packed)

6 ounces arugula (3 cups, packed)

1 small Yukon Gold potato, boiled

7 tablespoons grapeseed oil

5 tablespoons water

Salt and pepper to taste

Tabasco to taste

## SALAD

3 large Yukon gold potatoes, washed
    and peeled

3 ounces sprouts, plus extra for
    garnish (for example: radish, wheat,
    pea, alfalfa, etc.)

8 leaves Italian parsley, chiffonade

½ medium red onion, small dice

¼ cup grapeseed oil

2 tablespoons sherry or Banyuls
    vinegar

2 to 3 gratings fresh nutmeg

Salt and pepper to taste

To make the Sorrel-Arugula Emulsion: Clean sorrel and arugula; dry well. Remove stems and trim leaves if too large to make them easier to feed into a blender. In a high-speed blender, combine the cooked potato, grapeseed oil, water, salt, and pepper. Gradually add the sorrel and arugula leaves, and blend until smooth. Taste and adjust seasoning as needed. Finish with Tabasco sauce. Refrigerate until ready to use.

To make the Salad: Using a mandolin, slice potatoes into "linguine" strips. Do not rinse. Blanch strips immediately in well-salted boiling water for 45 seconds to 1 minute. (Be sure to use a sufficient amount of sea salt to ensure saltiness of water). Remove quickly and lay strips on a baking sheet lined with paper towels to absorb extra moisture. Place pan in the refrigerator until the strips are cooled. Clean and check sprouts. In a large bowl, combine cooled potato strips, sprouts, parsley, and onion. In a separate small bowl, whisk together grapeseed oil, vinegar, nutmeg, salt, and pepper. Pour over combined ingredients and toss gently with hands to prevent tearing of the delicate potato "linguine."

How to Plate: Arrange Salad in a mound in the center of a plate. Drizzle generously with Sorrel-Arugula Emulsion. Add extra sprouts on top to garnish.

# Warm Watermelon Salad with Tomatoes, Crushed Pistachios, and Aged Balsamic Vinegar

SERVES 4

1 ripe watermelon (about 5 pounds, preferably seedless)

6 pounds very ripe tomatoes

¼ cup olive oil, plus extra for drizzling

Fleur de sel and freshly cracked black pepper to taste

½ pound green pistachios, chopped or crushed, preferably not with a food processor*

½ cup aged (or reduced to a near syrup) balsamic vinegar

*As the pistachios are very rich in oil, the use of a food processor to chop or crush them will create more of a soft paste than the desired crunchy texture. It is preferable to use a chef's knife to chop or crush the nuts.

Preheat oven to 425 degrees F.

Slice watermelon into 1-inch-thick slices and place in a rectangle mold (or choose another shape such as a square or a ring cutter to cut to the desired size); set aside in the molds.

Cut a small X on the bottom of each tomato. Blanch them in boiling water until the cut skin of the tomatoes begins to peel away. Immediately plunge the tomatoes into ice water and peel the skins once cooled. Cut tomatoes in half and remove the inside pulp and seeds. Cut into ¼-inch slices and then into a small dice. Place the tomatoes in a bowl and season with oil, fleur de sel, and pepper.

Place watermelon slices, still in molds in order to keep it nicely packed, on a baking sheet. Season with fleur de sel, pepper, and a drizzle of oil. Using a slotted spoon, top the seasoned watermelon with a ½- to ¾-inch-thick layer of tomatoes. Lightly press the mixture with the back of a large spoon and cover the tomato layer with a light coating of the chopped or crushed pistachios. Bake at 425 degrees F until the pistachios start to brown lightly, approximately 3 to 5 minutes.

How to Plate: Using a squeeze bottle, generously drizzle with the aged balsamic vinegar, creating a zigzag pattern on the plate; and carefully place the watermelon onto the plate and remove the molds.

# Seasonal Vegetable Medley with Sautéed Tofu and Horseradish Broth

SERVES 4

## VEGETABLES AND SAUTÉED TOFU

2 leeks, trimmed to white part
  only, julienne

1 medium carrot, peeled, julienne

½ stalk celery, sliced thinly crosswise

1 stalk fennel, sliced thinly crosswise

1 medium cucumber, unpeeled, cut
  in half lengthwise, seeded, and
  sliced thinly

4 ounces (1 cup) haricots verts,
  ends trimmed

2 cups fresh or frozen soybeans

2 ounces soy sprouts

5 ounces fresh shiitake mushrooms

½ to ¾ cup grapeseed oil, for sautéing

1 pound firm tofu

¼ to ½ cup rice flour, for coating

3 to 4 tablespoons water

Salt and pepper to taste

2 tablespoons Dijon mustard

## HORSERADISH BROTH

Salt and pepper to taste

½ quart water

1 pound fresh horseradish, peeled
  and grated on a fine box grater
  or microplane

To make the Vegetables and Sautéed Tofu: Blanch each of the first seven vegetables separately until al dente. Immediately place in ice water to stop the cooking process. Drain and pat dry each vegetable separately. Clean and check the sprouts. Brush the mushrooms with a cloth or paper towel to clean them and then slice into quarters and sauté lightly with oil; set aside. Slice tofu into ½-inch slices and lightly flour with the rice flour. Sauté tofu in grapeseed oil until lightly browned; set aside. In a large sauté pan, combine all the blanched ingredients with the mushrooms and warm them gently with grapeseed oil and the water. When hot, season with salt and pepper and blend together with Dijon mustard.

To make the Horseradish Broth: Salt the water and bring to a boil. Place a strainer over a bowl and line it with a coffee filter or cheesecloth. Place horseradish and a dash of pepper in the strainer and pour boiling water over them. Check the broth in the bowl for seasoning and adjust as necessary. If horseradish flavor is too overwhelming, dilute to desired strength with additional hot water. Use this broth immediately (recommended for best flavor, bright and clear). If needed, cool down for later use.

NOTE: When reheating broth, to prevent a bitter taste, do not bring to a boil. Simply place broth into a pot and heat gently to warm.

How to Plate: In individual serving bowls, layer Sautéed Tofu on top of the vegetable medley. Pour Horseradish Broth around the vegetables. Garnish with celery leaves.

# Chilled White and Yellow Peach Soup, Poached with Beer and Lemon Verbena

SERVES 4

5 large yellow peaches

5 large white peaches

½ quart water

½ quart light beer

1 whole vanilla bean, split lengthwise

½ cup sugar

Juice from 1 lemon

1 orange, juiced

1 small bunch lemon verbena (or substitute mint)

Wash but do not peel the peaches. Cut them in half and remove the pits. Slice the peaches into ½-inch segments and reserve in a large bowl. Combine water, beer, vanilla bean, sugar, juices, and three-fourths of the lemon verbena (tie together to facilitate its removal later) in a pot and bring the liquid to a boil. Simmer gently for 5 minutes to fully absorb the flavor. Pour the hot liquid over the peaches in the bowl and allow to infuse for at least 2 hours while chilling in the refrigerator. When ready to serve, remove verbena and vanilla beans.

How to Plate: Pour peaches and liquid into individual bowls. Garnish the cold soup with a chiffonade of the remaining lemon verbena leaves.

Optional: Garnish with sliced toasted almonds and pieces of the vanilla bean (as shown in photo).

Washington Duke
Inn & Golf Club

Jason Cunningham
Executive Chef

# Jason Cunningham

*"While visiting an organic farm, a friend pulled a carrot from the ground and gave it to me. It was one of the greatest tastes I have ever had. The beauty of plant foods is congruent with appreciating such ingredients and combining them with each other as complements. It is truly at the core of what being a creative culinarian is all about."*

A graduate of Johnson & Wales University, Jason Cunningham received his culinary training on the island of Lanai in Hawaii and at two acclaimed Relais & Chateaux properties—Restaurant Million in Charleston, South Carolina, and Blantyre in Lenox, Massachusetts. In 1998, his European training earned him a finalist ranking in the Confrerie de Chaine des Rotisseurs' national commis chef competition at Johnson & Wales University in Charleston, South Carolina.

Since 2001, Cunningham has been creating "neo-American cuisine" at the award-winning Washington Duke Inn & Golf Club in Durham, North Carolina. His cooking style reflects his formal culinary training and his personal passion for American regional Asian, French country, and haute cuisine. Overseeing an extensive culinary team for planning and preparation of restaurant, banquet, meeting, special event, and in-room dining service, Cunningham's innovative dishes continue to impress the media and discriminating international palates. He has become a highly respected chef and an industry standard-bearer at one of America's most notable inns.

# Butternut Squash Soup

## SERVES 4

1 tablespoon extra virgin olive oil

1¼ cups diced sweet onion

½ cup diced carrot

¼ cup diced celery

1 large butternut squash, peeled,
  seeded, and diced

1 tablespoon peeled and minced
  fresh ginger

3 cups Vegetable Stock (recipe below)

1 bouquet garni (2 bay leaves,
  ½ teaspoon black peppercorns,
  2 sprigs thyme), bundled and
  tied in cheesecloth

Kosher salt to taste

## VEGETABLE STOCK

6 cups large-dice yellow onion

2 cups large-dice celery

1½ cups diced leeks (white parts only)

1 cup large-dice carrot

1 medium fennel bulb, diced

¼ cup dry white wine

2 tablespoons kosher salt

1 bunch Italian parsley, stems only

6 sprigs thyme

4 bay leaves

1 tablespoon whole black peppercorns

4 cloves garlic, crushed

2 gallons water

In a 2-quart saucepan, heat oil over medium heat and sweat the onion, carrot, and celery about 5 minutes, or until onion is translucent. Add the squash and ginger, and cook 5 minutes more. Add the Vegetable Stock, bouquet garni, and salt, and bring to a slow simmer. Cook until squash is tender.

Working in small batches, transfer the soup to a blender and purée until silky smooth. Place soup into another saucepan as each batch is puréed. Keep a small amount of additional Vegetable Stock warm on the side and use it to thin the soup, if necessary, as the soup can thicken as it cools slightly.

Return the soup to the stove over low heat to reheat and adjust seasoning. Can be refrigerated up to 5 days.

To make the Vegetable Stock: Combine the onions, celery, leeks, carrots, and fennel in a large saucepan and place over medium heat. Add the wine and salt. Cover the saucepan to sweat the vegetables until tender, about 10 minutes.

Add the parsley, thyme, bay leaves, peppercorns, garlic, and water, and bring to a simmer, uncovered. Reduce heat to slow simmer and cook for about 1 hour, or until flavorful. Strain the stock through a fine mesh sieve and chill immediately.

Reserve 3 to 4 cups for immediate use in the Butternut Squash Soup recipe as instructed. Fill pint-size freezer containers with the remaining stock and freeze up to 3 months.

NOTE: This recipe makes about 1³/4 gallons. Only 1 quart is needed for the Butternut Squash Soup (for 4 servings). It is wise to have vegetable stock on hand in the freezer for future use, up to 3 months, stored in handy pint containers. If you wish not to make extra, the recipe may be adjusted.

*Recipe continued on next page*

## GRANNY SMITH APPLE AND RADISH SLAW

1 Granny Smith apple

4 red radishes

½ lime, juiced

1 teaspoon extra virgin olive oil

Kosher salt to taste

## FRAGRANT GREEN HERB OIL

½ cup fresh Italian parsley, leaves only

¼ cup fresh basil leaves, tightly packed

¼ cup whole fresh chives

¼ cup fresh spinach leaves

3 cups canola oil

To make the Granny Smith Apple and Radish Slaw: Finely slice the apple and radishes using a Japanese mandolin. In lieu of a mandolin, use a very sharp chef's knife and thinly slice, then julienne. Combine the apple and radishes in a small mixing bowl. Add the lime juice, oil, and salt, and mix thoroughly.

NOTE: This will not keep well, so it must be prepared fresh or about 1 hour before serving for best results.

To make the Fragrant Green Herb Oil: Bring a 1½-quart saucepan of water to a boil; prepare a small bowl of ice water and place on the side. Using a strainer, blanch the herbs and spinach, and then shock in an ice water bath. Remove the herbs from the ice water as soon as they are chilled and pat dry with paper towels.

Transfer the herbs and spinach to a blender with 1 cup canola oil and purée. With the blender running, slowly add the remaining canola oil and allow this mixture to blend for about 1 minute.

Transfer the oil to a container and refrigerate for 2 to 3 hours to allow the solids to settle from the oil. Line a strainer with two layers of cheesecloth and place it over a bowl. Pour the herb oil through the strainer, being careful not to pour the solids, and allow it to drain through to the bowl; discard the solids.

How to Plate: Pour Butternut Squash Soup into shallow soup bowls. Garnish each with a mound of the Granny Smith Apple and Radish Slaw piled in the center. Finish the soup by dotting the Fragrant Green Herb Oil in a circle around the slaw.

NOTE: The leftover oil is delicious to use for salad dressings, pasta, and vegetables.

# Stuffed Baby Bell Peppers with Sunflower Seed Risotto, and Fava Bean and Carrot Purées

SERVES 4

### ROASTED BELL PEPPERS

4 baby red bell peppers

4 baby orange bell peppers

### FAVA BEAN AND CARROT PURÉES

2 large carrots, peeled

1 teaspoon kosher salt

½ teaspoon finely ground white pepper

2 to 3 cups Vegetable Stock (see page 133), divided

2 tablespoons olive oil, divided

1 cup fresh fava beans, shelled and blanched (if unavailable, use frozen)

To make the Roasted Bell Pepers: Char the peppers over an open flame or grill until the skin is black and blistered. Immediately transfer to a bowl and cover tightly with plastic wrap. Allow the peppers to cool slightly until they can be handled. Carefully remove the charred skin from the peppers with your fingers. Using a paring knife, carefully remove the stems and seeds, keeping the hulls of the peppers intact, and reserve warm. (Note that charring the peppers produces more flavor.) Handle peppers gently as they are fragile. If making for entertaining, make some extras in case there is a tear.

To make the Fava Bean and Carrot Purées: Preheat oven to 300 degrees F. Season carrots with salt and pepper, and place in baking dish with 1 cup Vegetable Stock. Wrap the dish tightly with aluminum foil and place in the oven; bake for 40 minutes, or until just tender.

Transfer the carrots and stock from the baking dish to a blender and purée until smooth. Add 1 tablespoon oil and adjust seasoning with salt and pepper. Add more Vegetable Stock as needed to achieve the desired consistency; reserve and keep warm.

Shell and then blanch fava beans in salted boiling water until just tender, about 1 minute.

Transfer to a blender and purée with ¼ cup Vegetable Stock and remaining oil. Adjust seasoning with salt and pepper and add additional Vegetable Stock as needed to achieve the desired consistency. The purée should be the consistency of very smooth applesauce. Reserve and keep warm.

*Recipe continued on next page*

## VEGETABLES

8 baby carrots

4 baby fennel bulbs

1 teaspoon kosher salt

½ teaspoon ground white pepper

¼ cup olive oil

12 fava beans

## RISOTTO

2 tablespoons olive oil

¼ cup finely minced shallot

1 cup arborio or carnaroli rice
   (short-grained round or semi-round)

4 cups Vegetable Stock (see
   page 133), warm

½ cup sunflower kernels, toasted

1 tablespoon chopped fresh
   thyme leaves

Salt to taste

## GARNISH

Beet greens or other available greens

To make the Vegetables: Peel and then cook the baby carrots in salted boiling water until tender, about 1½ minutes. Chill them in ice water and reserve.

Cook fennel bulbs in salted boiling water for 45 seconds, chill in ice water, and dry thoroughly. Season with salt, pepper, and oil. Just before serving, grill each side for 1 minute.

Cook the fava beans in salted boiling water for 30 seconds and chill in ice water. Remove immediately, dry, and reserve.

To make the Risotto: In a medium saucepan over medium heat, add the oil and lightly sauté shallot until tender. Reduce heat to medium-low and remove shallots with a slotted spoon, leaving oil in the saucepan; reserve. Add the rice to the pan and toast lightly, stirring constantly until it becomes aromatic, about 10 minutes. Return the shallots to the rice.

Stir in ¼ cup warmed Vegetable Stock. If the stock has become cold, it can shock the rice and become flaky instead of the creamy result desired. Continue to stir the rice. Once the liquid is almost absorbed, add ¼ cup more warm stock and continue to stir; repeat this process until the rice is tender and creamy.

Fold in the sunflower kernels and thyme. Adjust seasoning with salt only if needed. Note that seasonings will also come from the Vegetable Stock, so it is important to taste first and then adjust; remove from heat.

How to Plate: Spoon the Fava Bean and Carrot Purées onto each plate in long streaks side by side. Gently spoon heated Risotto into the Roasted Bell Peppers and place one of each color on each plate. Arrange the Vegetables between the stuffed peppers. Top one pepper with beet greens as a garnish or other greens on hand.

# Layers of Grilled Tofu and Marinated Eggplant with Rice Noodles, Sea Beans, Crispy Ginger, and Coconut Red Curry Emulsion

SERVES 4

### TOFU AND EGGPLANT

2 (8-ounce) packages extra-firm tofu

1 large eggplant

Kosher salt

1/2 cup mushroom soy sauce (Pearl River Bridge preferred)

1/2 cup sesame oil

1/4 cup rice wine vinegar

1 tablespoon peeled and minced fresh ginger

### COCONUT RED CURRY EMULSION

1 tablespoon canola oil

1/4 cup finely diced onion

1 clove garlic, chopped

1 teaspoon peeled and minced fresh ginger

1 teaspoon finely minced lemongrass (root end only)

1 teaspoon Penang red curry powder (or Madras Curry)

1/4 cup Vegetable Stock (see page 133)

1 (14-ounce) can unsweetened coconut milk

Kosher salt to taste

To make the Tofu and Eggplant: Cut the tofu into 8 slices, each about 1/3 inch thick. Line a baking sheet with paper towels and place the tofu on the pan in a single layer. Cover the tofu with additional paper towels and place another baking sheet on top. Place two dinner plates or other weights on top of the pan to gently press the tofu to help remove excess moisture for about 1 hour or more.

Wash the eggplant and dry with a towel. Cut the skin from the outside of the eggplant with a stainless steel knife to prevent reactions that can cause it to turn black. Slice the eggplant lengthwise into strips about 1/2 inch thick. Cut the strips into rectangles the same size as the sliced tofu. Place on paper towels arranged in a pan and sprinkle very lightly with kosher salt; reserve for about 1 hour to allow some of the water content to expend.

In a nonreactive bowl, combine the soy sauce, sesame oil, rice vinegar, and ginger, whisking thoroughly.

Remove the tofu slices from the "press," pat dry with a towel, and place in a very lightly oiled shallow baking dish to make it easier to remove for grilling. Rinse the salt from the eggplant slices, pat dry, and put them in the dish with the tofu. Reserve 1/4 cup of the marinade and pour the remaining marinade over the sliced eggplant and tofu, being sure they are well coated; marinate for 1 hour.

To make the Coconut Red Curry Emulsion: Place a nonreactive saucepan on the stove over medium-low heat. Add the oil and lightly sauté the onion until tender. Add the garlic, ginger, and lemongrass, and cook 2 to 3 minutes. Add the curry powder and cook, stirring frequently, for about 3 to 4 minutes, being careful not to burn the curry powder.

*Recipe continued on page 140*

## CRISPY GINGER TOPPING

1 (2-inch) piece gingerroot, peeled
1 cup canola oil

## TO FINISH

½ pound vermicelli rice noodles,
   cooked and chilled
12 sea beans*, soaked in ice water
   10 minutes and drained (if
   unavailable, consider using
   asparagus or French green beans)
Basil leaves for garnish

*Beans that are long, thin green stalks,
   commonly carried by rivers into the
   ocean with a resulting taste of sea salt.

Add the Vegetable Stock and cook, stirring frequently, and reduce liquid until a paste forms. Whisk in the coconut milk and bring contents to a slow simmer for about 5 minutes; remove from heat.

Transfer the contents to a blender and purée until smooth. Strain the sauce through a fine mesh sieve to remove any pulp, and then return the sauce to the stove over low heat. Adjust seasoning with salt and keep warm.

To make the Crispy Ginger Topping: Using a Japanese mandolin with the finest blade attachment, carefully push the ginger through lengthwise until completely cut. Heat oil in a small saucepan to 325 degrees F and sprinkle the ginger into the oil; fry until golden brown and just crisp, watching very closely. Remove the ginger from the oil quickly and allow to drain on a paper towel.

To Finish: Place the rice noodles in a bowl and toss with the remaining marinade from the tofu and eggplant; reserve.

Grill the sliced tofu and eggplant over medium-high heat for about 2 minutes on each side, carefully turning once on the diagonal to achieve the crisscrossed grill marks. Reserve in a warm oven.

How to Plate: Divide the rice noodles evenly among four plates. Top the noodles with a slice of eggplant and then place a slice of tofu on top of the eggplant; repeat with another slice of each. Spoon the warm Coconut Red Curry Emulsion around the stacks, garnish each plate with three sea beans, and top each stack with a pinch of the Crispy Ginger Topping and some basil leaves.

# Strawberry Lime Soup with Yerba Mate Sorbet

SERVES 4

### STRAWBERRY LIME SOUP

1 cup water

1 cup turbinado sugar (reduce sugar
   if strawberries are very sweet)

2 pints fresh ripe strawberries

3 limes, juiced

Salt to taste

### YERBA MATE SORBET

½ cup turbinado sugar

½ cup water

2 tablespoons yerba mate tea leaf

### GARNISH

4 strawberries, tops and bottoms
   trimmed

Fresh mint, for garnish

To make the Strawberry Lime Soup: Combine water and sugar in a nonreactive saucepan and bring to a boil. Remove from heat, chill until cold, and reserve. Place the fresh strawberries in a blender and purée thoroughly with the sugar syrup. Add the lime juice and salt. Purée until smooth and strain the soup through a fine mesh sieve.

To make the Yerba Mate Sorbet: Prepare a sugar syrup by combining the sugar and water in a saucepan and bring to a boil. Place the tea in a bowl and pour the sugar syrup over it. Allow to steep for 10 minutes; strain and chill until very cold, about 2 hours.

Using an ice cream maker, churn the tea according to the manufacturer's directions until desired consistency and place in the freezer.

How to Plate: Divide the soup among four shallow soup bowls. Place one strawberry in the center of the soup. Using two tablespoons, roll and shape the sorbet into a quenelle shape and anchor on top of the strawberry. Top with a mint leaf.

# Jean-Georges Vongerichten

*"Always begin simply, with the simplest classic ingredients, and from there the options for creating great dishes are limitless. I like combinations that are novel, even startling, yet appealing to anyone who likes to eat and sample new flavors."*

Jean-Georges Vongerichten is internationally known for his innovative and unconventional French-Asian cuisine. His impeccable culinary palate was acquired at an early age growing up in Alsace and tasting dishes that his mother and grandmother prepared for fifty employees in the family business. His sixteenth birthday present was a meal at the 3-Michelin star Auberge D'Lill. After training with Paul Haeberlin, Paul Bocuse, and Louis Outhier, he got an appointment at the Oriental in Bangkok. He's opened ten hotels around the world and, in 1986, was named executive chef at the Drake Swissotel in New York. At twenty-nine he was awarded his first four-star review in the *New York Times*.

In 1993, Vongerichten opened his first restaurant, Jo Jo. It won Best New Restaurant in *Esquire* and three stars in the *New York Times*. Vongerichten then opened Vong with additional Vong outposts in London, Hong Kong, and Chicago. Vong introduced explosive Thai-French flavors inspired by his years working in the Orient. In 1997, Vongerichten opened his flagship restaurant, Jean-Georges, in the Trump International Hotel and Tower. It quickly earned four stars in the *New York Times*, three Michelin stars, a James Beard Foundation Best New Restaurant award, and a prestigious Relais Gourmand designation. Vongerichten's culinary brand continues to grow through ventures with Starwood Hotels & Resorts Worldwide Inc. and Catterton Partners. He is the author of four books *Simple Cuisine, Jean Georges: Cooking at Home with a Four Star Chef, Simple to Spectacular,* and *Asian Flavors of Jean Georges*. He has appeared on numerous TV shows and is master cook for *Food & Wine* magazine and chef in residence for *CITY* magazine and oversees eighteen restaurants worldwide.

# Chilled Watermelon Gazpacho

SERVES 8 TO 10

## CHILLED GAZPACHO

2 quarts watermelon purée (15 pounds watermelon)

2 medium red bell peppers, seeded

2 medium English cucumbers

1 pint cherry tomatoes

1 teaspoon chopped Thai chile

2 tablespoons red wine vinegar

Salt and white pepper to taste

## GARNISH

1 red bell pepper, blanched and shocked, small dice or small dice watermelon

1 English cucumber, mostly peeled, small dice

1 yellow onion, small dice

1 cup micro purple basil leaves

To make the Chilled Gazpacho: Cut watermelon in half and scoop out, removing seeds. Purée by pushing through a mesh sieve or by using a blender; reserve.

In a blender, purée the bell peppers, cucumbers, tomatoes, and chile. Strain through a mesh sieve to remove pulp. Add vinegar and season with salt and pepper. In a large bowl, mix the purées together until well blended. Adjust seasonings to taste, and then chill.

How to Plate: Place about 2 tablespoons of each garnish in the corner of a soup bowl. Slowly pour desired amount of Chilled Gazpacho into the center of the bowl and then serve immediately.

NOTE: Recipe can be adjusted per yield need.

# Charred Corn Ravioli, Cherry Tomato Salad and Basil Fondue

SERVES 5 (3 RAVIOLI PER SERVING)

## CORN RAVIOLI

3 cobs corn

⅓ cup chopped shallots

1 Thai chile, minced (or more, if preferred)

1 teaspoon olive oil, more if needed

1 cup soy creamer, adjusted during cooking

1½ tablespoons minced fresh rosemary

Salt and pepper to taste

1 package eggless wonton wrappers, approximately 30

## TOMATO SALAD

1 cup quartered cherry tomatoes

1/4 cup thinly shaved shallots

1/2 cup basil, chiffonade

1/4 cup red wine vinegar

2 tablespoons olive oil

1 teaspoon salt

## BASIL PURÉE

1 pound (8 to 10 cups) basil, washed

Olive oil

Salt and pepper to taste

To make the Corn Ravioli: Remove husks from corn. Grill the corn cobs until well charred. Remove corn from cobs (about 1 cup) and reserve. Sweat shallots and chile in oil. Add corn and mix well. Slowly add creamer in four parts (as done when making risotto), stirring constantly until corn is completely cooked and glazed. Add mixture to a food processor and barely pulse until only half smooth and half chunky. Remove to a bowl, mix in rosemary, and season with salt and pepper.

Fill center of wonton wrappers with a scant tablespoon of pulsed corn mixture. Brush edges of wrapper with water, and then top with another wrapper and seal.

Bring a large saucepan of water to a simmer. Poach ravioli in simmering water just to cook the wrapper. Gently lift from the water with a slotted spoon and set aside, keeping warm in the oven and covered with plastic to keep moist.

To make the Tomato Salad: Toss tomatoes, shallots, and basil in a bowl. Mix in vinegar, oil, and salt; reserve.

To make the Basil Purée: Blanch basil quickly in boiling water. Squeeze excess water from basil, place in a blender; cover with oil, and purée on high until bright green. Pour into bowl placed over ice to shock and end cooking process, preserving the green color. Season with salt and pepper. Set aside.

## CORN

2 cobs corn, kernels removed for
    serving with ravioli

2 cobs corn, kernels removed to
    add to Basil Purée

Olive oil for sautéing

2 tablespoons cold soy margarine

## GARNISH

½ cup baby basil for garnish

To make the Corn: In a small saucepan, bring a small amount of lightly salted water to a boil, add kernels from 2 cobs, and gently cook for about 3 minutes; drain. Set aside and keep warm.

Sauté corn from remaining cobs in oil until tender, then add water to almost cover. Add soy margarine and emulsify by whisking, giving texture, flavor, and a glossy look. Combine with the Basil Purée. It should now be creamy and broth-like, not thick, and should be bright green.

How to Plate: Cover the bottom of a soup bowl with the basil-corn purée. Place a large spoonful of corn kernels in the center. Place three Corn Ravioli in the bowl, top with Tomato Salad, and sprinkle with baby basil.

# Grilled King Oyster Mushrooms and Avocado Carpaccio with Charred Jalapeño Oil

SERVES 4 TO 6

## GRILLED KING OYSTER MUSHROOMS

1½ pounds King Oyster mushrooms
  or portobello mushrooms
Fresh thyme sprigs
½ teaspoon minced Thai chile pepper
2 teaspoons salt
¼ cup olive oil

## CHARRED JALAPEÑO OIL

1 tablespoon grilled jalapeños, seeded
  and stems removed
½ cup olive oil
⅛ teaspoon salt

## AVOCADO

Juice of 3 limes
4 firm, ripe avocados, peeled
  and pitted

## GARNISH

Salt to taste
Lime juice
8 to 10 fresh sprigs of thyme, stripped
  of leaves

To make the Grilled King Oysters: Place whole mushrooms in a glass casserole dish and top with a few thyme sprigs, chile, and salt. Drizzle oil over top and cover with plastic wrap. Place dish in a warm place for 30 minutes. Heat a grill pan and grill mushrooms each side until tender. Remove from grill and cool for 15 minutes. Slice the mushrooms into thin strips.

To make the Charred Jalapeño Oil: Put jalapeños, oil, and salt in a blender. Purée until smooth and strain through a sieve to remove pulp; set aside.

To make the Avocado: Lightly sprinkle lime juice over the avocadoes to keep from oxidizing while preparing the plating.

How to Plate: Warm oval or oblong serving plates. Thinly slice the Avocados. On a piece of parchment paper that is slightly larger than the serving plate, alternate 8 mushroom slices and 7 avocado slices, beginning and ending with a mushroom slice. Note that other amounts can be used if desired. Invert onto the serving plate that has been warmed and further warm briefly in a 250-degree F oven for 2 minutes. Remove and brush liberally with the Charred Jalapeño Oil, sprinkle delicately with salt, drizzle with lime juice, and sprinkle thyme evenly over dish.

# Crispy Tofu with Sesame Dressing and Lilybulb Radish Salad

### SERVES 6

TEMPURA BATTER

⅔ cup cold water

2 teaspoons sherry vinegar

2 teaspoons sesame oil

1 teaspoon grapeseed oil

1 teaspoon salt

⅔ cup rice flour

⅛ teaspoon baking powder

⅛ teaspoon baking soda

To make the Tempura Batter: Mix the water, vinegar, and oils in a bowl; add salt, flour, baking powder, and baking soda. Gently mix until batter is smooth. The batter will only last for 1 hour.

## SESAME VINAIGRETTE

5 tablespoons grapeseed oil

3 tablespoons olive oil

2 tablespoons mustard oil

2 tablespoons roasted sesame oil

½ cup sesame seeds

4 tablespoons Dijon mustard

½ cup rice wine vinegar

3 tablespoons lime juice

3 tablespoons soy sauce

¼ teaspoon chopped fresh Thai
   chile, or to taste

2 teaspoons salt

## SALAD

2 parts sea beans, string beans, or
   Thai green beans, washed, trimmed,
   blanched, and shocked

2 parts baby radishes, washed,
   trimmed, and cut into quarters

1 part lilybulbs, trimmed and
   separated, charred a la minute
   (lightly blackened in a dry hot pan)

1 part young ginger, 2-inch julienne

1 part lime segment, small dice

Lavender flowers, picked and
   separated

## TOFU

6 (2-ounce) pieces firm or
   extra-firm tofu

Extra virgin olive oil for frying

Salt and white pepper to taste

Rice flour for dredging

## GARNISH

2 tablespoons toasted sesame seeds

To make the Sesame Vinaigrette: Combine the oils in a bowl. Toast the sesame seeds in a nonstick skillet until golden brown. While the seeds are still hot, add to blender with mustard, vinegar, lime juice, soy sauce, chile, and salt; blend until almost smooth. Stream in the oil mixture slowly and purée; set aside.

To make the Salad: Toss all ingredients together and set aside.

To make the Tofu: Pat tofu very dry. Heat a large skillet with oil for frying. Season tofu with salt and pepper, dredge in rice flour, and dust off excess flour. Coat tofu in the Tempura Batter. Deep-fry until crisp and golden brown; drain on paper towels.

How to Plate: Pour Vinaigrette into the center of each plate. Place crisp Tofu on top and gently top with the Salad. Sprinkle with toasted sesame seeds and serve.

# Strawberry Salad with Strawberry–Red Wine Sorbet

SERVES 8

## STRAWBERRY–RED WINE SORBET

1 pound strawberries, hulled
   and quartered
½ cup dry red wine
1 cup sugar
1 vanilla bean
Juice of 1 lemon

## STRAWBERRY SALAD

1 quart strawberries (small wild
   strawberries, if possible)
½ to 1 cup confectioners' sugar,
   as desired for sweetness
1 lemon, zested
1 lime, zested

## GARNISH

1 lemon, zested
1 lime, zested
Vanilla bean seeds

To make the Strawberry–Red Wine Sorbet: Combine the strawberries, red wine, and sugar in a bowl and stir. Split the vanilla bean lengthwise in half and scrape out the seeds. Mix all of the ingredients in a bowl, including vanilla bean pod, and let set for 45 minutes. Remove pod and purée the mix in a blender. Pour mixture into an ice cream maker and freeze according to the manufacturer's directions.

To make the Strawberry Salad: Hull and cut strawberries lengthwise in half or quarters, depending on the size. Combine strawberries, sugar, and zests in a bowl to macerate for 1 to 2 hours in the refrigerator.

How to Plate: In a shallow bowl with a wide rim, place a spoonful of Strawberry Salad. Make a quenelle of Strawberry–Red Wine Sorbet using two tablespoons rolled together and place on top of the salad. Sprinkle lemon and lime zest over top and onto the rim of the bowl. To decorate and add more flavor, rub a few inches of vanilla bean seeds along the rim or lip of the bowl and serve immediately.

# Crisp Chocolate with Sautéed Bananas, Fresh Figs, Blackberry Coulis, and Brandied Cherries

SERVES 6

*Johnny Iuzinni, Pastry Chef (James Beard 2006 Outstanding Pastry Chef in U.S.)*

## CHOCOLATE DISKS

14 to 18 ounces dark bittersweet
 chocolate

## CHOCOLATE SAUCE

2 cups water

1⅓ cups sugar (organic cane
 sugar preferred)

½ cup plus 1 tablespoon plus
 1 teaspoon cocoa powder, sifted

3 ounces 70% bittersweet chocolate

1 cup plus 3 tablespoons vanilla
 soy milk

## BLACKBERRY COULIS

½ pint fresh blackberries

2 tablespoons sugar (organic cane
 sugar preferred)

½ lime, juiced and zested

**To make the Chocolate Disks:** Temper the chocolate and then spread very thinly on a Silpat or sheet of acetate. Once chocolate is almost set, cut disks using a circle cutter, perhaps 2 to 2½ inches in diameter, that has been dipped in warm water and dried off. Once disks have been cut, place a piece of parchment paper on top and invert the whole sheet. Place a sheetpan on top to weigh down the layers and allow them to fully set—it's best if left overnight at room temperature. When set, carefully remove tray, peel back the plastic, and place chocolate disks someplace cool and humidity free. Do not place in the refrigerator.

NOTE: You will need 4 disks per serving.

**To make the Chocolate Sauce:** Bring water and sugar to a boil. Whisk in cocoa powder. While constantly whisking, bring mixture back to a boil. Add chocolate and soymilk, and then reduce to a simmer. Remove from heat and cool while whisking periodically until the sauce has thickened. Strain through a fine strainer and chill.

NOTE: Yields 4 cups, which is more than needed for this recipe. Adjust accordingly if a smaller amount is desired.

**To make the Blackberry Coulis:** Purée the blackberries, sugar, juice, and zest in a blender. Strain through a fine mesh strainer and chill.

*Recipe continued on following page*

## BRANDIED CHERRIES

1 cup sugar (organic cane sugar
   preferred)

1 cup water

¼ cup fresh lemon juice

2 cinnamon sticks

2 whole star anise

4 whole allspice, or ¼ teaspoon
   ground allspice

5 pounds fresh or frozen sour cherries

1½ cups good-quality brandy

## SAUTÉED BANANAS

2 tablespoons granulated sugar

⅛ teaspoon salt

1 banana, sliced about ¼ inch thick

1 teaspoon soy margarine

1 tablespoon dark rum (chef prefers
   Meyer's Rum)

## GARNISH

6 to 8 fresh ripe figs, washed and
   sliced about ¼ inch thick

Silver leaf for garnish

To make the Brandied Cherries: Bring sugar, water, and lemon juice to a boil. Reduce heat and add cinnamon sticks, star anise, allspice, and cherries; simmer for 10 minutes. Remove from heat and add brandy. Allow to cool, and then place into a jar and store in refrigerator for several months.

NOTE: Yields about 1 gallon of cherries, which is more than needed for this recipe. Adjust accordingly or keep extras on hand.

To make the Sautéed Bananas: Place a sauté pan over medium heat and add sugar and salt. When sugar begins to caramelize, stir the pan to promote even more. Add banana and toss to coat. Add the margarine and toss to coat. Tossing helps the bananas to retain their shape as opposed to handling them with a utensil. Remove pan from the flame and add rum. Carefully return pan to the fire, ignite the alcohol, and then toss until the alcohol is almost burned off in order to retain some rum flavor. Slide bananas onto a plate to cool. Be sure to do this process quickly, as you do not want the bananas to be too soft.

*Alternative method:* If using an electric stove or if you are uncomfortable with flaming, sprinkle rum onto bananas after cooking as they are cooling on the plate.

How to Plate: Place a large spoonful of cold Chocolate Sauce just off-center on each plate. Place the first Chocolate Disk on the edge of the sauce to keep it from sliding. Place 2 or 3 slices of room-temperature Sautéed Bananas on the disk, and then place another disk of chocolate on top with 2 or 3 slices of fresh fig. Place a third disk of chocolate over fig slices, and then repeat with another layer of bananas and 1 more disk of chocolate. (To have the disks slightly off-set as the "tower" is built, place each disk slightly backward from the one below it, and then anchor the back of the tower with a large fresh blackberry or piece of fig to prop the top disks securely.) Spoon a drop of Chocolate Sauce on the top disk and garnish with a piece of silver leaf. Add 2 or 3 Brandied Cherries and drops of the Blackberry Coulis on each side to finish.

NOTE: This recipe will take overnight steps.

# John Besh

*"No matter what you cook, cook it from the heart. Imagine every dish you prepare is being served to your lover!"*

John Besh grew up in southern Louisiana, and his cooking is deeply rooted in the traditions and flavors of the bayou. At an early age, he learned the essentials of Louisiana's rich culinary traditions by working in commercial kitchens. He followed his palate around the world, exploring the far-flung ingredients that now infuse his French cuisine at Restaurant August. Besh attended the Culinary Institute of America and, following apprenticeships in Germany and France, he led a squad of infantry marines in combat during Operation Desert Storm as a non-commissioned officer of the United States Marine Corps Reserve.

Since Hurricane Katrina, Besh has changed the way America thinks about food. He has renewed his previous commitment to buying locally to help invigorate the city and a food culture he loves. He served more than 3,000 meals daily to the St. Bernard Parrish civil servants and workers of local refineries and has helped to rebuild the venerable Willie Mae's Scotch House in the Treme neighborhood. He has also served as educational director of the Louisiana Restaurant Association, is a member of the Southern Food Alliance, and has served as a board member of the Southern Food and Beverage Association. In 1999, *Food & Wine* magazine named John Besh one of the Top 10 Best Chefs in America. In 2006, the James Beard Foundation named him Best Chef: Southeast, and he was victorious as the first New Orleans chef to compete against Mario Batali on Food Network's *Iron Chef. Gourmet* has ranked Restaurant August  as 22nd in its Top 50 Restaurants in the United States, and Gayot has named it a Top 40 Restaurant in the U.S. His other restaurants in New Orleans are Besh Steak in Harrah's New Orleans Casino, Lüke, and La Provence. He is working on his first cookbook, *My New Orleans.*

# August Chop Salad

3 golden beets

3 Chioggia beets

3 red beets

1 cup rice wine vinegar

½ cup sugar

1 cup whole chanterelle mushrooms

6 baby carrots, different sizes and
colors

6 baby turnips

1 small Yukon gold potato, peeled and
punched out with circle cutter

6 stalks asparagus

1½ quarts canola oil, for blanching
artichokes

2 artichokes, cleaned and choke
removed

1 bulb fennel

2 small radishes

1 Japanese eggplant

1 cup pomegranate seeds

½ grapefruit, sectioned

1 satsuma orange, sectioned

1 seedless cucumber (English or
hothouse), peeled and scooped
into small balls

1 cup sunflower sprouts

1 cup pea sprouts

1 sprig fresh dill

1 sprig fresh chervil

## VINAIGRETTE

½ cup champagne

½ cup white wine vinegar

2½ cups olive oil

Salt to taste

Place each type of beet in separate pots of water and bring to a simmer. Allow to simmer until fork tender. While beets are cooking, make a marinade by placing vinegar and sugar in a separate pot and warm until sugar has dissolved; remove from heat. Remove beets from water and allow to cool before peeling. Once peeled, place beets in separate bowls with some marinade for at least 4 hours.

Using a large 8-quart pot, bring salted water to a boil and blanch the mushrooms, carrots, turnips, potato punch outs, and asparagus in that order until each are al dente. Place into ice water to cool quickly; reserve.

In a 3-quart saucepot over medium heat, bring the oil to 360 degrees F. Blanch the artichoke in the oil until browned on all sides. Cut each artichoke into six pieces.

Slice fennel and radishes on a slicer or with a sharp knife as thinly as possible. Slice eggplant and grill on a well-oiled grill. Cool and cut into bite-size pieces. Save drippings and add to the vinaigrette, if desired.

To make the Vinaigrette: Place the champagne and vinegar in a mixing bowl and slowly whisk in the oil. Season with salt. Note that this is a broken vinaigrette and will need to be mixed again before being added to the salad.

How to Plate: Remove beets from marinade and divide evenly among 6 plates. Toss the carrots, turnips, eggplant, asparagus, fennel, mushrooms, artichokes, and radishes in Vinaigrette separately, and then scatter over the plates. Distribute pomegranate seeds, grapefruit sections, orange sections, and cucumber balls among the plates. Lightly coat the sunflower and pea sprouts with Vinaigrette and lay on top of each salad. Garnish with the dill and chervil.

# Fall Vegetables Three Ways and Chanterelle Risotto

SERVES 6

### SWEETENED SWEET POTATOES

1 large sweet potato, peeled and diced

½ cup sugar cane syrup

1 sprig fresh thyme

Salt to taste

### TRUFFLED CAULIFLOWER

1 head cauliflower

3 tablespoons olive oil

1 cup soy milk

2 tablespoons truffle oil

1 tablespoon rice wine vinegar

Salt to taste

Micro greens

### BABY TURNIPS AND GREENS

6 baby turnips with greens attached

2 cloves garlic, minced

1 tablespoon minced shallot

1 tablespoon olive oil

Salt to taste

1 stalk salsify, shaved with peeler and
　fried (parsnips can be substituted)

To make the Sweetened Sweet Potatoes: In a medium saucepan, bring lightly salted water to a boil. Add sweet potato to blanch in order to set the color and soften slightly. Drain and then add to a sauté pan with the sugar cane syrup and thyme, allowing syrup to glaze the sweet potato for about 8 minutes, or until fork tender. Season potatoes with salt. Gently spoon into four small serving bowls.

To make the Truffled Cauliflower: Cut 6 nice cross-sections of cauliflower florets to make a chip shape. Sear in olive oil and drain on a paper towel.

Rough chop the remaining cauliflower and add to a pot of salted water, simmering until tender. In the meantime, heat the soy milk in a saucepan. Drain cauliflower and combine with soy milk in a food processor to purée.

Mix the vinaigrette by whisking together truffle oil, vinegar, and salt.

Spoon the purée into the bottom of four small serving bowls and garnish with a cauliflower chip. Top with micro greens that have been tossed in the vinaigrette.

To make the Baby Turnips and Greens: Bring salted water to a boil in a medium saucepan. Remove greens from turnips and wash. Blanch turnips until fork tender; cool and peel.

Using a heavy-bottomed saucepan, sweat garlic and shallot in oil, making sure not to brown. Add turnip greens and sauté until soft. Season with salt.

Place sautéed greens in the bottom of four small serving bowls. Warm turnips, if needed, and place on top. Garnish with fried salsify.

## RISOTTO WITH BATTER-FRIED ASPARAGUS AND MUSHROOMS

5 cups vegetable stock

1 tablespoon plus 1 cup olive oil

2 tablespoons chopped onion

1 cup Arborio rice

1 cup dry white wine

1 quart canola or other frying oil

1 cup cold water

1 cup flour

Salt to taste

6 stalks asparagus, washed and cut into bite-size pieces

6 chanterelle mushrooms, cleaned and cut into bite-size pieces

Chives to garnish

To make the Risotto with Batter-Fried Asparagus and Mushrooms: Heat stock in a saucepan and bring to a simmer. Heat 1 tablespoon olive oil in a large sauté pan over medium heat, adding onion and sautéing until soft. Add the rice and cook for 1 minute, making sure to stir constantly. Add white wine and cook until completely absorbed. Add ½ cup warm vegetable stock and cook until absorbed, stirring constantly. Once all the vegetable stock is absorbed, add another ½ cup. Repeat this process until all the stock has been used. Remove from heat and let set, covered, for a few minutes. Take off lid and stir in remaining olive oil. Season with salt.

Heat canola oil in a 1½-quart saucepan to 330 degrees F. Mix together the water, flour, and a pinch of salt. Do not overmix or batter will become greasy. Coat asparagus and chanterelles in batter and fry in the oil to just before browning. Gently lift out with a mesh or slotted spoon and drain on paper towels.

How to Plate: Spoon risotto into four small serving bowls and top with fried asparagus and mushrooms. Top with strips of chives quickly dipped in the frying oil. Place one each of the four serving bowls on one large plate or tray in a tight arrangement to serve as one course.

# Chocolate Cake with Chocolate Truffle Molten Center and Gluhwein—Stewed Berries with Spiced Wine

## CHOCOLATE TRUFFLE MOLTEN CENTER

8 ounces bittersweet chocolate

¼ cup cocoa butter (coconut oil/butter can be used)

2 tablespoons favorite liqueur (optional)

## CHOCOLATE CAKE

1 cup flour

5 tablespoons sugar

3 tablespoons cocoa

¾ teaspoon baking soda

¼ teaspoon salt

¼ vegetable oil

¾ teaspoon vanilla

2 teaspoons vinegar

5 tablespoons coconut milk

¼ cup confectioners' sugar for dusting, approximately

## GLUHWEIN-STEWED BERRIES

3 pounds fresh berries (such as blackberries, blueberries, cherries, raspberries, strawberries, etc.)

2 cups Pinot Noir (or similar red wine)

½ cup sugar

1 orange peel

1 bay leaf

1 cinnamon stick

1 vanilla bean

2 tablespoons arrowroot, dissolved in 4 tablespoons water

To make the Chocolate Truffle Molten Center: Melt the chocolate in a double boiler or very carefully in the microwave for a few seconds. Once the chocolate is melted, whisk in the cocoa butter until smooth. (If desired, add favorite liqueur now.) Allow the mixture to cool. Use a tablespoon measure to scoop out the chocolate mixture and roll it into a ball. Repeat this process six times. Place truffles on parchment paper, cover, and reserve in the freezer.

To make the Chocolate Cake: Preheat oven to 425 degrees F. Lightly grease six foil cupcake tins (about 3¼ inch diameter and 1¾ inch high) and dust with cocoa.

Sift together the flour, sugar, cocoa, baking soda, and salt. Whisk together the oil, vanilla, vinegar, and coconut milk. Combine mixtures together until smooth.

Pour batter into prepared tins, about ⅔ full. Press the reserved chocolate truffles into the center of the cupcake tins. Bake at 425 degrees F for 15 to 20 minutes. Remove from oven and run a knife between the tin and the cake; turn out onto a tray or plate. Keep warm while making Gluhwein-Stewed Berries; or make berries before the cake and keep warm. However the order, cake should be warm when served.

To make the Gluhwein-Stewed Berries: Rinse berries and put aside. In a heavy saucepan over medium heat, combine the wine, sugar, orange peel, bay leaf, cinnamon stick, and vanilla bean, and bring to a boil. Add arrowroot mixture to thicken. Simmer for 2 minutes. Add berries and then set aside to cool.

NOTE: Gluhwein is the German term for mulled wine.

## SPICED WINE

6 cups red wine (Pinot Noir
   or similar wine)

½ lemon peel

1 orange peel

1 cinnamon stick

1 clove, crushed

2 peppercorns, crushed

2 cardamon pods

2 ounces Kirschwasser (cherry brandy)

## GARNISH

1½ cups fresh assortment of berries
   for garnish, approximately

6 sprigs mint

To make the Spiced Wine: Combine the wine, lemon and orange peels, cinnamon stick, clove, peppercorns, and cardamom pods in a saucepan and warm. Do not boil. Add the Kirschwasser and remove from heat.

How to plate: If Chocolate Cakes have cooled, briefly warm in the oven. On a dinner or dessert plate, place desired amount of Gluhwein-Stewed Berries upon which the cupcake will sit. Before placing cupcake, lightly dust the tops with confectioners' sugar using a hand strainer; top the center with an arrangement of fresh berries and garnish with a sprig of mint. Add a wine glass containing the Spiced Wine to the plate and serve immediately.

# Jose Andres

*"For me, the farmer's market has become a Sunday ritual. Just as they do in Spain today, the smaller organic farmers are introducing the city crowd to new fruits and vegetables. I find inspiration for wonderful tapas dishes every week."*

Spanish-born Jose Andres began his formal culinary career as an intern with Ferran Adria at El Bulli. Today, with seven restaurants in the Washington, D.C., area, he has been praised by the *New York Times,* named Chef of the Year by *Bon Appétit,* and won Rising Star Chef and Best Chef: Mid-Atlantic awards from the James Beard Foundation.

Born in a small farming town outside of Barcelona, Spain, Andres enjoyed the fresh local produce at an early age and tended the fire while his father prepared paella for his family on weekends. When he was fifteen, he worked in a three-person restaurant and first met Ferran Adria, who was considered the best chef in the village. After culinary school in Barcelona, Andres was privileged to work at El Bulli with Adria as his mentor. Military service in the navy brought Andres to America, and he worked in Spanish restaurants in New York and Washington, D.C., before opening Jaleo in 1993. Jaleo has become a platform for Spanish food traditions and the social aspects of sharing. In 2007, Andres opened Minibar, an innovative six-seat restaurant within a restaurant, and published *Tapas,* his first cookbook.

# White Asparagus with Oranges and Olives

SERVES 1

### BLACK OLIVE OIL

1 cup black olives

1½ cups extra virgin olive oil, divided

### WHITE ASPARAGUS

4 fresh white asparagus spears

4 orange segments

2 black olives, cut in half

1 tablespoon Black Olive Oil
  (recipe above)

2 tablespoons Sherry Dressing
  (recipe below)

### SHERRY DRESSING

¼ cup sherry vinegar

¾ cup extra virgin olive oil

Salt to taste

### GARNISH

Salt

Micro greens

To make the Black Olive Oil: In a blender, purée the olives and ½ cup oil. In a bowl, mix the remaining oil and black olive purée.

NOTE: This will make more than is needed for this recipe. Keep on hand for use with many dishes, or cut the recipe to a smaller amount while keeping the proportions. Keep refrigerated.

To make the White Asparagus: Gently peel the stem of the asparagus and set aside. Bring salted water to a boil. Drop in the asparagus and cook for 3 minutes. Remove and shock in an ice water bath to stop the cooking process; cool.

Peel an orange, removing all the white pith; remove segments by cutting on each side of the white membrane just to the center of the orange.

To make the Sherry Dressing: In a small bowl, whisk together all the dressing ingredients.

How to Plate: Carefully toss the asparagus, orange segments, Sherry Dressing, and salt. Remove the asparagus and cut in half. Place on a small plate in log cabin style. Place orange segments and black olives around the asparagus. Drizzle Black Olive Oil around the plate and garnish with micro greens.

# Green Bean Salad with Cherry Tomatoes and Pearl Onions

*Ensalada de Judías Verdes y Cebolletas*

SERVES 1

3 ounces green beans

1 bunch onion leaves (pieces)

6 cherry tomatoes

1 sprig fresh thyme

12 sliced almonds, toasted

2 tablespoons Sherry Dressing
   (see page 166)

6 edible micro flowers

Bring a saucepan of salted water to a boil. Blanch green beans to the al dente stage. Shock in an ice water bath to preserve color and stop the cooking process.

How to plate: In a bowl gently toss together green beans, onion leaves, tomatoes, thyme, almonds, and Sherry Dressing. Place in small bowl and garnish with sea salt and edible flowers.

# Sautéed Cauliflower with Olives and Dried Fruits

*Coloflor con Aceitunas y Fruitos Secos*

SERVES 4

1½ tablespoons vegetable oil

4 ounces cauliflower, cut into
   bite-size pieces

1 sprig fresh thyme

5 dates, cut into quarters

4 black olives

4 green olives

2 tablespoons Pedro Ximenez*

Pimenton

*A very distinct Spanish dessert wine,
a sweet sherry.

Heat oil in a sauté pan. Sear the cauliflower and thyme, being sure to equally caramelize all sides. Add dates and olives, and sauté for about 1 minute. Deglaze with the Pedro Ximenez and burn off the alcohol.

How to plate: In a small serving bowl, place the cauliflower mixture and sprinkle with pimenton.

# Skewer of Watermelon and Tomato

*Pinchito de Sandia y Tomate*

SERVES 1

1 teaspoon pimenton

5 cherry tomatoes

5 (1-inch) cubes watermelon

2 tablespoons Lemon Dressing
(recipe below)

Sea salt to taste

Edible micro flowers

## LEMON DRESSING

1 tablespoon fresh lemon juice

1 teaspoon lemon zest

¼ cup extra virgin olive oil

1 tablespoon sherry vinegar

Bring water to a boil in a saucepan. Cut a small X on the bottom of each tomato and drop into the boiling water for 15 seconds. Remove from water and shock in ice water. When tomatoes are cooled, gently peel each tomato.

In a small bowl, whisk together all the dressing ingredients.

How to plate: Gently push a tomato on each of five skewers, sliding through until 1 inch of the skewer is showing. Slide watermelon cubes onto skewer under each tomato. Place in a row on a plate, side by side. Drizzle with the Lemon Dressing and sea salt. Artfully place the flowers on top of the tomatoes near the skewers.

# Avocado Cotton Candy

*A cotton candy machine for home use will be needed to make this recipe. Follow manufacturer's directions, but generally the procedure should be the following. Do not attempt in a moist or humid environment.*

1 avocado

1 cup Corn Nuts

Salt to taste (Malden salt is
  chef's favorite)

Sugar, based on the machine
  instructions

1 lemon or lime

Cut the avocado in half, remove the pit and carefully scoop out the avocado with a tablespoon; or if pliable enough, peel away the outer skin. Cut the avocado halves into roughly $1/2$-inch cubes. Refrigerate while preparing Corn Nuts.

Using a coffee grinder, pulverize the Corn Nuts to an instant-coffee texture and spread thickly on a plate. Place one avocado cube on each skewer, or as many as desired. Lightly salt, being careful to realize that the Corn Nuts might already be salty. The salt is important to balance the sweet taste of the cotton candy. Adjust to taste. Roll each skewered avocado piece in the Corn Nut powder, or sprinkle on the cotton candy at the end with the lemon or lime zest.

Turn the machine on to warm for about 4 minutes or at the direction of the machine's instructions. Usually pour 1 tablespoon of sugar into the reservoir of the spinning disc. The cotton candy will come out in a thin thread at first. Once it comes in a steady stream, catch the candy with a skewer of avocado in hand, wrapping the avocado with a twist of the wrist. Or, as at the carnival, use a make-shift paper cone to collect a large fluff of the candy and then wrap some around the avocado with tongs. Do not wrap too heavily as it will make it too sweet.

As each one is done, stick the other end of the skewer in a holder or a large vase of sugar for anchoring. Be careful the cotton candy does not touch each other as they can stick together.

Using a microplane or zester, top the cotton candy with a light dusting of lemon or lime zest, or additional Corn Nuts.

Note that the size can be smaller than the pieces in the photo and might be more manageable to start. Make only what will be consumed immediately.

Amway Grand Plaza

Executive Chef CMC

# Josef Huber

*"Nature is still the best cuisine. Cook with seasons when it is in full bloom, as its yield from the earth need little help. Eat raw or eat well-prepared foods, and treat food with care and respect for its own amazing flavor offerings."*

Josef Huber is known for combining multiethnic cuisine and traditional cooking with a focus on accessible ingredients that are comforting yet challenging and new. He realized his culinary calling at the age of sixteen when he was an apprentice at the 5-Star, 5-Diamond Elisabeth Park in his homeland of Salzburg, Austria. The experience led to an international tour of luxury properties that shaped his culinary identity and destiny. He worked with world-renowned chefs Paul Bocuse, Roger Verge, Charlie Palmer, and Gaston Lenotre, and at The Imperial and Bristol Hotel in Vienna, Wild Coast Sun Hotel and Casino in South Africa, Regency in Bangkok, French Bistro in Orlando at the Epcot Center, The Breakers Hotel in Palm Beach, and The Mandarin Oriental in Hawaii and San Francisco.

In 1997, Huber was named executive chef at the historic Amway Grand Plaza Hotel in Grand Rapids, Michigan. His culinary responsibilities include ten restaurants and lounges, four ballrooms, forty function spaces, and all culinary spectacles at the DeVos Place Convention Center that connects to the Amway Grand Plaza. Under his leadership, the hotel has achieved the only AAA 5-Diamond restaurant designation in Michigan for The 1913 Room. Huber's recipes have been featured in *Gourmet, Palm Beach Post, Food Arts, San Francisco Chronicle and Examiner,* and *Business Journal.* He has also appeared on cooking shows, developed a 2004 cooking video series titled *Culinary Extraordinaire,* and actively supports the March of Dimes and the Make-A-Wish Foundation.

# Chocolate-Stuffed Michigan Cherry French Toast with Rice Krispies served with Peach-Strawberry Compote and Maple Syrup

SERVES 4

## MICHIGAN CHERRY FRENCH BREAD (MAKES 4 LOAVES)

10 cups bread flour (do not use self-rising)

4 tablespoons sugar

1 teaspoon salt

1 teaspoon dry instant yeast

1 teaspoon ground cinnamon

1 cup powdered egg replacer (chef's preference is Red Mill or Ener-G)

2½ cups lukewarm water

⅓ cup vegetable oil

1 cup chopped dried cherries

## STRAWBERRY-PEACH COMPOTE

1 cup fresh peaches, cut into wedges

1 cup quartered fresh strawberries

2 tablespoons brown sugar

To make the Michigan Cherry French Bread: In a large mixing bowl, combine the flour, sugar, salt, yeast, cinnamon, and egg replacer. Add lukewarm water and oil, and combine. Knead thoroughly for about 10 minutes to form a smooth, silky-looking dough. Add cherries and knead for another minute, or until incorporated. Form the dough into a large ball. Cover with a damp cloth and let the dough rest for 15 minutes at room temperature. Divide the dough into 4 smaller balls. Cover with a damp towel and let them rest for 5 minutes.

Sprinkle some flour on a work surface to prevent the dough from sticking. Roll the dough into loaves that are about 12 to 14 inches long. Place loaves on a baking sheet lined with parchment paper. Preheat oven to 375 degrees F. Let the loaves rise again for 45 minutes, or until the desired height has been reached. Bake for 20 to 25 minutes, or until golden brown, yielding a hollow sound when tapped. Cool for 2 hours before slicing. The leftover bread will keep in your bread box for several days, or wrap with plastic wrap and freeze for later.

NOTE: This is a popular bread in the Michigan area, celebrating their high production of cherries. If you don't have time to make the bread, other store-bought bread can be substituted.

To make the Strawberry-Peach Compote: Place all compote ingredients into a small saucepan over low heat and bring to a simmer for about 10 minutes. Check to make sure peaches are soft and not crunchy. Remove from heat and cool in refrigerator.

*Recipe continued on page 178*

## DIPPING BATTER

2 cups vanilla soy milk

1 cup freshly squeezed orange juice

6 tablespoons Grand Marnier liqueur

2 teaspoons ground cinnamon

2 tablespoons egg replacer (Red
   Mill or Ener-G)

4 tablespoons maple syrup

## CHOCOLATE-STUFFED
## FRENCH TOAST

12 squares organic bittersweet
   chocolate

24 (½-inch) slices Michigan Cherry
   French Bread (see page 176)

4 cups Rice Krispies

½ cup powdered sugar

To make the Dipping Batter: Prepare the batter by whisking together the soy milk, orange juice, Grand Marnier, cinnamon, egg replacer, and maple syrup. Pour the batter into a pan large enough to accommodate the bread slices.

To make the Chocolate-Stuffed French Toast: Place a chocolate square on 12 bread slices. Take the other bread slices and place them on top of the chocolate slices like a sandwich. Place the "sandwich" slices in the Dipping Batter and let soak for 20 seconds, turning them over after 10 seconds or so. Place Rice Krispies in a bowl, and then coat the bread slices with Rice Krispies.

Heat a griddle or sauté pan over medium heat and coat with vegetable spray. Place the prepared sandwiches on the hot griddle and cook until the bottom turns golden brown; flip and cook on the other side. When the toast is crispy on the outside, remove from heat and place on paper towels. Place some powdered sugar into a fine sieve and lightly dust the bread.

How to Plate: Spoon ½ cup Strawberry Peach Compote on bottom of a deep-dish bowl. Unevenly stack three 2-slice "sandwiches" or desired amount of French toast on top of each other. Dust with powdered sugar again and drizzle with maple syrup. *Guten Appetit!*

# Homemade Garlic Tortillas with Tofu Scrambled Eggs, Roasted Seven-Tomato Salsa, and Fresh Guacamole

SERVES 4

## SEVEN-TOMATO SALSA

6 cups diced assorted heirloom tomatoes, or best ripe tomatoes available (chef uses seven different varieties)

1 shallot, diced small

1 clove garlic, chopped

1 jalapeño pepper, sliced lengthwise, seeded, and minced

½ cup extra virgin olive oil, divided

2 tablespoons chopped fresh cilantro

Celtic sea salt and freshly ground black pepper

1 lemon, juiced

Dash of hot sauce (Cholula Hot Sauce is chef's favorite)

## GARLIC TORTILLAS

2 cups instant corn masa (chef prefers Maseca)

1⅛ cups room-temperature water

1½ tablespoons chopped garlic

2 tablespoons chopped fresh cilantro

Salt and pepper to taste

1 quart vegetable oil

**To make the Seven-Tomato Salsa:** Preheat the oven to 450 degrees F or use the broiler. Cut the tomatoes into roughly ³/4-inch-size pieces. Mix the chopped tomatoes with the shallot, garlic, jalapeño, and ¼ cup oil. Place on a roasting tray and put in oven. Roast the tomatoes for about 10 minutes. The tomatoes have more flavor if the tomato skins become slightly charred; remove from oven and let cool. The tomatoes should be soft and mushy. If smaller pieces of roasted tomato are desired, give them a rough chop at this point. Transfer into a bowl and season with cilantro, remaining oil, salt, pepper, lemon juice, and hot sauce.

**To make the Garlic Tortillas:** Mix the masa, water, garlic, cilantro, salt, and pepper thoroughly for 2 to 3 minutes, or until the dough forms into a firm ball. If the dough is too dry, add 1 to 2 tablespoons water. Divide the dough into 12 balls and cover with a damp cloth to keep moist. Flatten the dough between your hands. Place each flattened ball between two sheets of parchment paper and roll out, or put into a tortilla shell press until tortilla measures 6 to 7 inches. Carefully peel off the paper on one side. Heat a cast-iron skillet over high heat and add tortilla, allowing the paper on the other side to assist in lowering the tortilla into the skillet as it peels off. Cook the tortilla on each side for about 30 seconds, or until it turns a nice brown color; remove from the heat. Cover the tortillas to keep them soft and pliable.

In a medium sauté pan, heat the oil. Cut tortilla shells into quarters and fry until crispy. Remove from oil, season with salt, and set aside on paper towels.

*Recipe continued on next page*

## MACADAMIA NUT SOUR CREAM

1 cup macadamia nuts, soaked in
water for 6 hours or longer

3 tablespoons unsweetened
coconut flakes

1 tablespoon fresh lemon juice

Pinch Celtic sea salt

2 tablespoons apple cider vinegar

½ cup water, or less

## FRESH GUACAMOLE

1 ripe avocado

½ fresh lime or lemon, juiced

Celtic sea salt, to taste

Dash Cholula hot sauce

## TOFU SCRAMBLED EGGS

1 pound extra-firm tofu

1 clove garlic, crushed

½ teaspoon turmeric

Pinch Celtic salt

Black pepper, freshly ground

1 tablespoon olive oil

## GARNISH

1 (16-ounce) can refried beans

1 (15-ounce) can black beans

16 scallions, grilled

Oil for grilling

Salt to taste

To make the Macadamia Nut Sour Cream: Measure all ingredients into a high-speed blender and blend until very smooth. Stop to scrape the sides with a rubber spatula. Note that the amount of water can differ depending on the soaked nuts and the coconut moisture. Perhaps start with a small amount of water and add as needed for the desired consistency for smooth sour cream.

To make the Fresh Guacamole: Cut the avocado in half. Remove the pit; scoop the avocado from the skin with a spoon. Place into a bowl. Mash with a fork and season with lime or lemon juice, salt, and hot sauce.

To make the Tofu Scrambled Eggs: In a large bowl, break up the tofu into small pieces. Add garlic, turmeric, salt, and pepper, and mix well. Heat oil in a sauté pan over medium heat. Add mixture to the pan and sauté until the consistency of scrambled eggs.

To make the Garnish: Remove refried beans and black beans from cans and warm each in two small saucepans; reserve. Heat a grill over high heat. In a large bowl, toss scallions in oil and salt. Place scallions on the grill using tongs and grill until softened and charred in patches, about 4 to 5 minutes total. Transfer to a platter and reserve.

How to Plate: On a dinner plate, place three tablespoons of Seven-Tomato Salsa in the center. Sprinkle the salsa with some black beans. Place a fried Garlic Tortilla shell on top of the salsa and beans, and spoon the Tofu Scrambled Eggs on top of the tortilla. Place another tortilla shell leaning tall alongside. With two small spoons, shape the Fresh Guacamole, Macadamia Nut Sour Cream, and refried beans into quenelles, placing each on a corner of the plate. Garnish with 3 or 4 grilled scallions, draping artfully on top of the scrambled tofu and tortillas.

# Ethnic Chic Far East "Breakfast"

### SERVES 4

## RED PEPPER PURÉE

3 red bell peppers, halved, seeded, and stemmed

2 tablespoons extra virgin olive oil, divided

## TOFU SALMON STEAK

1 pound extra-firm tofu

1 clove garlic, crushed

Celtic sea salt, to taste

1 tablespoon finely chopped fresh ginger

3 tablespoons Red Pepper Purée (recipe above)

¾ cup panko breadcrumbs (pure white Asian breadcrumbs)

¼ cup black sesame seeds

¼ cup white sesame seeds

## VEGETABLE RICE ROLLS

4 cups sushi rice

4 cups cold water

1 cup rice vinegar

¼ cup mirin rice wine

¼ cup sugar

1 cucumber

1 red bell pepper

1 ripe avocado

4 sheets nori

To make the Red Pepper Purée: Rub with 1 tablespoon extra virgin olive oil and grill over a very hot grill until the skin turns almost black. While still hot, wrap in plastic wrap and let cool for easier peeling (and to keep the cooking process continuing, which intensifies the flavor). Remove the blackened skin by rubbing with fingers or with a small knife and discard. Purée the peppers in a blender until smooth. Season with a tablespoon of olive oil. Adjust seasonings.

To make the Tofu Salmon Steak: Crumble the tofu into small pieces in a mixing bowl. Add the garlic, salt, ginger, red pepper purée, and breadcrumbs. Mix very well and set aside for 30 minutes or so to let the breadcrumbs absorb the moisture. The mixture should be firm enough to form patties. If it is too soft, add more breadcrumbs. The tofu mixture should be about the same pink color as salmon. Divide mixture into four mounds and shape into oval patties; coat with sesame seeds.

Heat a medium nonstick skillet over medium heat (to ensure the sesame seeds do not brown too much before steaks are cooked through) and pan-sear the steaks until cooked all the way through, about 4 to 5 minutes on each side.

To make the Vegetable Rice Rolls: Soak rice in a bowl of cold water, mixing occasionally with your hands. As the water becomes cloudy, drain and rinse. Repeat this process until the water runs clear. Allow the rice to drain in a strainer for 30 minutes or so. Add the rice and 4 cups cold water to a heavy medium-size saucepan. Cover with a tightly fitting lid. Do not lift the lid at any point until the rice is finished cooking, or steam will escape and it will not cook properly. Turn the heat to high until the rice boils; cook for 2 minutes. Next, reduce heat to simmer and cook for another 5 minutes. Turn off the heat and let stand, covered, for 15 minutes to finish the cooking process.

*Recipe continued on next page*

In a small saucepan combine the vinegar, mirin, and sugar, and heat over medium heat until hot. Do not boil.

Remove the rice from the saucepan into a large bowl. Gently fold half of the vinegar mixture into the rice. Taste and, if necessary, fold more vinegar mixture into the rice. Cover with a damp towel and let rest for about 20 minutes.

Peel and seed the cucumber; cut into strips about the size of pencils, about 7 inches long. Cut the red bell pepper in half, remove seeds, and cut into strips the size of pencils as well. Cut the avocado in half, remove the seed, and remove the flesh from the skin with a spoon. Cut into strips.

For making an inside-out sushi roll, place a nori sheet on a bamboo rolling mat used for sushi, glossy side down, and spread sushi rice evenly over it. Cut plastic wrap the same size as the sushi mat and cover the rice. Pick up the mat, placing a hand over the plastic wrap, and carefully turn over so that the nori is on top. Place back on mat about three slats from edge closest to you.

Place cucumber, bell pepper, and avocado in a row across the center of the nori from edge to edge, or left to right. Pick up the mat and plastic wrap closest to you and place fingers over fillings to hold them as you roll mat forward tightly, wrapping rice and nori around fillings. Press gently and continue rolling to complete roll. Gently press, pat to shape, and seal roll. Unroll mat and transfer to cutting board.

Wipe a sharp knife with a damp towel. Through the plastic wrap, cut the roll in half and then cut the halves in half again. Then, cut each quarter in half to make 8 equal pieces, wiping knife after each cut. Gently remove the plastic wrap from each piece.

NOTE: This can possibly make 32 rolls depending on size, but only 18 pieces are needed for 4 servings if using three rolls per serving. Adjust accordingly.

## MUNG BEANS

2 cups dried mung beans, soaked
    overnight in water

¼ teaspoon Celtic sea salt, plus more

4 tablespoons extra virgin olive oil

Pepper to taste

## MISO SOUP

4 cups purchased miso soup

Fresh spinach greens

Carrot strips, very thin

## GARNISH

2 cups purchased wakame salad

4 teaspoons pickled ginger, rolled
    into rose shapes

4 teaspoons wasabi, shaped into
    quenelle shapes

Soy or tamari sauce

To make the Mung Beans: Place the soaked mung beans in a medium pot with cold water and ¼ teaspoon salt and bring to a boil. Reduce the heat to a simmer and let cook until tender, about 15 to 25 minutes. Strain and season with olive oil, salt, and pepper.

To make the Miso Soup: Boil water and add miso powder per package instructions, or buy miso and follow instructions. Add fresh spinach to wilt in the hot soup. Garnish with carrot strips.

How to Plate: On a long narrow plate, arrange the Tofu Salmon Steak on one side. On the other side arrange three Vegetable Rice Rolls in a row. Add a quenelle of wasabi and rose-shaped pickled ginger on each side of the rolls. Lightly drizzle entire plate with soy or tamari sauce.

Serve the Mung Beans, Miso Soup, and wakame salad in small matching bowls, side by side, with chopsticks.

NOTE: You can fill the rolls with whatever you like. Try sautéed spinach, mushrooms, wakame salad, kim-chee, etc. Even for your sweet cravings, try filling the rolls with fresh mango and papaya, and use peanut butter to substitute the wasabi. The options are endless.

# Austrian Wellness Muesli with Almond Milk, Cinnamon, and Fresh Berries

SERVES 4

## ALMOND MILK

1 cup raw sliced almonds, soaked
    in water for 6 hours
3 tablespoons coconut flakes
½ stick cinnamon bark
5 cups water, distilled preferred
¼ cup agave syrup or maple syrup
1 tablespoon flax seed oil

## MUESLI

1 cup spelt flakes, organic preferred,
    or favorite cereal
1 cup Almond Milk (recipe above)
1 tablespoon agave syrup
1 cup mixed field berries or
    favorite fruit
1 whole orange, cut into segments
1 whole apple, julienne

## CARAMEL SUGAR CAGES

¾ cup sugar
¼ cup plus 2 tablespoons water
½ teaspoon corn syrup

To make the Almond Milk: Mix all ingredients in a high-speed blender and purée until the consistency is similar to milk. Strain through a chinois strainer or other fine sieve. Store any extra in the refrigerator to drink or use for smoothies, chai tea, or other cereal dishes during the week.

To make the Muesli: In a large bowl, mix all the ingredients together. Let sit for about 20 minutes until the milk's flavor soaks into the ingredients.

To make the Caramel Sugar Cages: In a small saucepan, add sugar, water, and corn syrup and bring to a boil. Cook without stirring, until sugar turns amber. (To be sure it is boiled to the right stage, attach a candy thermometer to the saucepan without having its end touch the bottom of the pan and cook until the mixture reaches a temperature of 311 degrees F.)

Pour into a 10-ounce microwaveable glass bowl (or large custard cup) and set aside. Use glass bowls of desired size for cages, not larger than the size of serving plates, and spray insides with a nonstick cooking spray. Gently stir caramel with a teaspoon until even in texture. Fill spoon with caramel and drizzle evenly over inside of bowl. Repeat until bowl is covered; set aside for 5 minutes to cool. Work quickly with remaining bowls. If mixture becomes too thick, reheat for a few seconds in the microwave.

Using a sharp knife, clean the top edge of the bowl of any caramel. To remove cage from bowl, place your thumbs on each side of and inside the bowl, pushing in a circular motion until caramel cage releases. Very gently flip out of bowl. Cages can be stored in an airtight container in a cool, dry place for a day or two.

NOTE: Based on the size of bowl chosen, you may have more caramel than needed for four cages.

How to Plate: Carefully arrange the Muesli on shallow plates or bowls, add a drizzle of Almond Milk, if desired, and top with the Caramel Sugar Cages.

# Marcus Samuelsson with Johan Svensson, Carina Ahlin, and Jimmy Lappalainen

*"I try to create interesting flavors and build them to contrast in several different ways. Plant food is a big part of that whether it is through herbs or through greens that are available at various times throughout the year. Respecting ingredients is the most important thing."*

Marcus Samuelsson is the co-founder and chief creative director of Townhouse Restaurant Group, a restaurant management and consulting company with projects in the U.S. and Europe, including New York City's Aquavit, Ringo, AQ Café, August, and Merkato Fifty Five. He is the author of four successful cookbooks, most recently *Soul of New Cuisine: The Discovery of the Foods and Flavors of Africa.* He is also the host of *The Inner Chef with Marcus Samuelsson* on the Discovery Home channel and the recipient of two James Beard Foundation awards—Rising Star Chef (1999) and Best Chef: New York (2003). At the age of thirty-seven, he received numerous accolades in the *New York Times,* including the youngest chef ever to receive a three-star review, as well as in the *Chicago Tribune* and *Washington Post.*

A graduate of the Culinary Institute in Gothenburg, Sweden, Samuelsson apprenticed in Switzerland, Austria, and France before coming to the U.S. In 1995, he was hired as Aquavit's executive chef, and only four months later, he acquired three stars in the *New York Times.* He has been celebrated as one of The Great Chefs of America by the Culinary Institute of America, has an honorary doctorate degree from Johnson & Wales University, and is an ambassador for the U.S. Fund for UNICEF. He also serves on the Board of Directors of Careers through Culinary Arts Program (C-CAP) and, since 2005, has been Visiting Professor of International Culinary Science at the Umea University of Restaurant and Culinary Arts.

# Salsify Noodles with Pickled Fennel

*Johan Svensson, Executive Chef, Aquavit, NYC*

SERVES 4

## SALSIFY

2 pounds salsify, cleaned and salted
  (parsnips can be substituted)

4 quarts boiling water

4 quarts ice water to cool noodles

## PICKLED FENNEL MIX

2 cups water

1 cup sugar

1/2 cup Swedish vinegar

4 cherry tomatoes, skins removed

8 green grapes

1 stalk fennel, thinly sliced

## COCONUT-SAFFRON SAUCE

2 shallots, chopped

2 cloves garlic, chopped

1 large piece, about 2 inches,
  young ginger, chopped

2 tablespoons olive oil

3 tablespoons white port

1 quart coconut milk

2 sprigs tarragon

1 pinch saffron

Salt and pepper to taste

## GARNISH

Tarragon leaves

Pepper to taste

To make the Salsify: Use a potato peeler to make noodles of the salsify until nothing is left and the noodles look like tagliatelle in long strips. Boil the salsify until al dente, about 4 minutes. Transfer to the ice water to stop the cooking process and to cool.

To make the Pickled Fennel Mix: Mix the water, sugar, and vinegar until sugar is dissolved.

Cut an X on the bottom of the cherry tomatoes and blanch quickly in boiling water; peel the tomatoes and add to the vinegar mix. Slice the grapes lengthwise and add the fennel. Soak with the vegetables for 1 hour or more.

To make the Coconut-Saffron Sauce: Sweat shallots, garlic, and ginger in oil; deglaze with white port. Add coconut milk, tarragon, and saffron; cook 10 minutes. Pour into a blender and blend until smooth; strain and season with salt and pepper.

How to Plate: Using both hands, lift a handful of Salsify noodles from the cooling water and lower the bottom of noodles onto a paper towel to slightly drain; place noodles in the middle of a shallow bowl with wide rim. Add a pickled tomato and several grapes, then top with a few slices of pickled fennel. Gently pour about 1/4 cup Coconut-Saffron Sauce into the bottom of the bowl around the noodles. Garnish with a few tarragon leaves and a sprinkle of pepper, if desired.

# Eggplant and Vanilla Purée, Chinese Broccoli, and Fried Tofu "Cutlet"

*Jimmy Lappalainen, Executive Chef, Ringo, NYC*

SERVES 4

14 ounces soft tofu

6 eggplants, regular variety (double amount if using Japanese eggplants)

½ cup vegetable oil

1 vanilla bean

Salt and white pepper to taste

1 pound Chinese broccoli

½ cup eggless tempura flour*

⅓ cup water

2 cups breadcrumbs

1 clove garlic, thinly sliced

8 cups vegetable oil for deep-frying

*If eggless tempura flour is not available, make it by lightly combining 3 cups all-purpose flour, 1 teaspoon baking powder, and 2 cups ice cold water. Do not overmix.

GARNISH

Variety of small greens, or as pictured: popcorn shoots, baby red shiso, baby tatsoi shoots, and baby beet shoots

Preheat oven to 350 degrees F. Cut the tofu into rectangular pieces and then set aside in the refrigerator.

Cut the eggplant in half lengthwise. Rub the flesh side with oil and put on a roasting pan. Bake until golden brown and the flesh is soft, about 30 to 40 minutes. Cool slightly and then scoop out flesh and discard the skin. Cut the vanilla bean in half lengthwise and scrape out the seeds. Mix the eggplant and vanilla seeds in a blender to a smooth purée. Season with salt and white pepper. Reserve in a small saucepan for warming before use.

Wash broccoli, trim the leaves, and then slice the stems thinly on a bias and set aside.

Mix the tempura flour and water, dip the cut tofu into the mixture and then into the breadcrumbs; set aside.

Warm eggplant and vanilla purée over medium heat.

In a separate pan, heat 2 tablespoons oil over high heat and sauté the sliced broccoli stems for about 1 minute. Add the sliced garlic and broccoli leaves. Sauté for about 2 minutes, add salt and white pepper to taste.

Drop the breaded tofu into the deep fryer and fry until golden brown. If you don't have a deep fryer, fill a saucepan with 8 cups oil and heat it to 350 degrees F to fry.

How to Plate: Place a large spoonful of the eggplant purée onto one side of each plate. Pile broccoli onto the center of the plate, slightly overlapping the eggplant, and then prop a tofu "cutlet" against the broccoli. Garnish with fresh greens, such as popcorn shoots, baby red shiso, or other micro greens and sprouts of choice.

# Yuzu Marinated Fruit Salad with Carrot-Mango Sorbet

*Carina Ahlin, Pastry Chef*

SERVES 6

SIMPLE SYRUP
2½ cups sugar
2 cups water

To make the Simple Syrup: Combine sugar and water in a saucepan and bring to a boil until sugar dissolves; cool.

## YUZU MARINADE

16 kumquats

1 cup sugar

1 cup orange juice

⅓ pineapple

1 Asian pear

1 papaya

1 tablespoon unsalted yuzu
   or lime juice

1 teaspoon lemon juice

12 leaves fresh mint, chopped

## CARROT- MANGO SORBET

2 cups mango purée, purchased
   or prepare*

2 cups fresh carrot juice, purchased
   or use a juicer to prepare

2 cups Simple Syrup (recipe on
   facing page)

½ cup water

⅓ cup fresh lemon juice

*Make mango purée by peeling, seeding,
and slicing about 6 mangoes and
place in a blender with ½ lemon,
juiced. Blend while adding a tablespoo
of water at a time until reaching the
desired purée consistency.

## MANGO SAUCE

1 ripe mango

2 tablespoons Simple Syrup (recipe
   on facing page)

1 teaspoon fresh lemon juice

## GARNISH

2 lemons or oranges

To make the Yuzu Marinade: Cut the kumquats in half and bring them to a boil in water to cover. Shock them in ice water to remove any bitterness and to retain color. Simmer the kumquats in the sugar and orange juice until they are clear. Let cool and remove the meat and seeds.

Cut off the skin from the pineapple. Peel the pear and the papaya. Dice all the fruit into bite-size pieces. Combine yuzu and lemon juice. Add to the fruits and toss lightly. Add mint and set aside.

To make the Carrot-Mango Sorbet: Blend mango purée, carrot juice, Simple Syrup, water, and lemon juice. Freeze in ice cream maker according to the manufacturer's directions.

To make the Mango Sauce: Peel and cut the mango from the seed and blend in a blender until smooth; add Simple Syrup and lemon juice and blend until very smooth.

How to Plate: Place layers of the Yuzu Marinade in a ramekin and unmold onto one side of each plate. Create a little "bowl" with two sections of a lemon or orange, removed from between the white membranes of the fruit, by placing the wider part on the outside. Place a scoop of Mango Carrot Sorbet on top. Drag a spoonful of Mango Sauce across the plate and then serve.

# Matthew Kenney

*"Plant-based ingredients provide endless rewards to a serious chef's kitchen—not only providing fresh and vibrant flavor, they bring us closer to the environment, nutrition, and seasonality, all of which are essential building blocks for well-rounded, creative cuisine."*

Matthew Kenney grew up on the coast of Maine, but his attraction to the energy of New York and his passion for cooking and restaurants led him to enroll in the French Culinary Institute. After culinary stints at La Caravelle and Alo Alo, at twenty-eight, he opened his first restaurant in 1993. Kenney's was an overnight success and he became widely known for his dynamic ideas and innovative regional Mediterranean cuisine. In 1994, *Food & Wine* magazine named him one of the ten best new chefs in America, and he received his first Rising Star Chef nomination from the James Beard Foundation. In 1997, he published his first cookbook, *Matthew Kenney's Mediterranean Cooking,* and by 1998 he had opened four new restaurants in New York.

Kenney shifted his focus to regional American cuisine in 1999 and expanded his culinary empire from New York to Atlanta and Portland, Maine. He also launched Matthew Kenney Catering and Events, introduced a line of gourmet products called Modern Fare, and published a second book, *Matthew Kenney's Big City Cooking.* In 2002, he adopted a raw vegan and organic lifestyle and refocused his entire culinary career in a direction he had been leaning toward for a number of years. Soon after, he opened three business ventures—Pure Food & Wine, The Plant, and Blue/Green. He co-authored a raw food cookbook, *Raw Food Real World* and also launched a new company, Organic Umbrella, through which he is currently working on promoting organic living projects throughout the world, including London, India, and the United States. He recently completed two upscale cookbooks, *Everyday Raw* and *Plant Food.*

# Zaru Somen with Sweet Dashi

### SERVES 2

## SWEET DASHI

1 cup water

1 cup Nama Shoyu, or less for
 a less salty taste

2 tablespoons dried dulse

1 tablespoon dried wakame

¼ cup brown rice vinegar

2 tablespoons raw agave nectar

1 tablespoon lime juice

## SOMEN

¾ cup young Thai coconut meat

## GARNISH

¼ teaspoon black sesame seeds

¼ teaspoon Sachimi chile spice,
 or other chile spice

1 tablespoon finely sliced scallions

To make the Sweet Dashi: In a blender, blend water, Nama Shoyu, dulse, and wakame until smooth. Strain through a fine mesh sieve into a medium-size bowl and whisk in remaining ingredients. Store in refrigerator until ready to serve. (Note that this will make more than 2 servings, but it's good to have for more dishes later.)

To make the Somen: To open a young Thai coconut, lay it on its side, securing it so it won't roll. Hold a cleaver high over the coconut and bring it down sharply near the top (pointed side) of the coconut, cutting through the shell. Drain the coconut water and reserve for later use. Finish cutting off the top to get to the meat.

Use the back of a spoon to pry the meat from the sides of the coconut and trim any shell residue with a paring knife. Lay the pieces of coconut flat on a cutting board and slice strips to make the noodles. Slice coconut meat into very thin, uniform "noodles."

NOTE: Coconut meat will range from very soft and thin to thicker and firmer. Only the firmer meat will make good noodles, so it's good to get some extra coconuts; but you can save the softer meat for other uses, and it will keep well in the freezer. One young coconut will yield from ½ to ¾ cup coconut meat.

How to Plate: When ready to serve, pour ¼ cup Sweet Dashi in the bottom of two small serving bowls. Place equal amounts of Somen in each serving bowl with Sweet Dashi. Top each with a sprinkle of sesame seeds, Sachimi, and scallions. Serve immediately.

# Sushi and Nigiri

SERVES 2

## SUSHI "RICE"

4 cups jicama, peeled and roughly
    chopped
2 teaspoons sea salt
2 tablespoons rice wine vinegar
1½ tablespoons raw agave nectar

## CHIPOTLE MAYONNAISE

¼ cup macadamia nuts, soaked
    1 to 2 hours
½ small dried chipotle chili, soaked
    1 to 2 hours
2 tablespoons soaking water from
    chipotle chile, more if needed
¼ cup cold-pressed extra virgin
    olive oil
Sea salt to taste

## ELEPHANT ROLL

½ portobello mushroom, stemmed and
    sliced about ½ inch thick
1½ teaspoons Nama Shoyu
1 tablespoon cold-pressed sesame oil
1 sheet untoasted nori
½ cup Sushi "Rice" (recipe above)
2 tablespoons Chipotle Mayonnaise
    (recipe above)
¼ cup torn baby spinach
¼ red bell pepper, sliced into strips
1 whole scallion

To make the Sushi "Rice": Process jicama in a food processor until rice-like consistency is achieved; do not overprocess. Dry mixture between paper towels or strain through a cheesecloth to remove excess moisture.

In a medium bowl, whisk together the salt, vinegar, and nectar. Add jicama rice and toss until well-combined. Sprinkle mixture over a dehydrator screen and dehydrate 1 to 2 hours to remove excess moisture.

To make the Chipotle Mayonnaise: Blend all ingredients in a high-speed blender until very smooth. Store in the refrigerator until ready to use.

To make the Elephant Roll: In a medium bowl, toss the mushroom slices with Nama Shoyu and sesame oil. Spread marinated slices on dehydrator screens and dehydrate 40 minutes, or place in a warm area for 1 to 2 hours, or until soft.

Lay the nori sheet, shiny-side down, on a bamboo mat. Spread Sushi "Rice" over three-fourths of the nori, leaving about 2 inches at the top end of the nori sheet uncovered.

In the middle of the rice, horizontally spread the Chipotle Mayonnaise, top with torn spinach, bell pepper slices, whole scallion, and marinated mushrooms. Roll sushi tightly and wet end of nori to ensure it holds securely.

Transfer to a cutting board; cut off the ends with a very sharp or serrated knife, then cut into 6 equal pieces.

*Recipe continued on page 202*

## BANANA-BANANA ROLL

1 teaspoon umeboshi plum paste

½ teaspoon wasabi powder

1 sheet untoasted nori sheet

½ cup Sushi "Rice"

¼ medium banana, peeled

2 tablespoons fresh watercress

1 tablespoon fresh cilantro leaves

2 tablespoons green papaya, peeled
   and julienned

10 to 12 whole enoki mushrooms

## NIGIRI

4 small shiitake mushrooms,
   stems removed

½ teaspoon Nama Shoyu

1 teaspoon cold-pressed sesame oil

1 cup Sushi "Rice"

4 thin slices fresh mango

1 untoasted nori sheet (optional)

## PICKLED GINGER

2 tablespoons fresh ginger, peeled
   and finely sliced

¼ cup raw apple cider vinegar

1 tablespoon raw agave nectar

1 tablespoon beet juice or shredded
   beet (optional)

To make the Banana-Banana Roll: In a small bowl, mix the umeboshi plum paste and wasabi powder until well combined.

Lay the nori sheet, shiny-side down, on a bamboo mat. Spread umeboshi-wasabi mixture in a horizontal line over middle of the nori sheet. Spread Sushi "Rice" over three-fourths of the nori and umeboshi-wasabi, leaving about 2 inches at the top end of the nori sheet uncovered.

Cut banana in half and quarter lengthwise, then place in middle of the Sushi "Rice" horizontally. Next to the banana, place watercress, cilantro, papaya, and mushrooms. Roll sushi tightly and wet end of nori to ensure it holds securely.

Transfer to a cutting board; cut off the ends with a very sharp or serrated knife, then cut into 6 to 8 equal pieces. Stick a few enoki mushrooms into the top of each cut piece to garnish.

To make the Nigiri: Toss shiitake caps in Nama Shoyu and sesame oil, and let marinate in a warm place for 10 to 15 minutes.

Place about 2 tablespoons Sushi "Rice" in the palm of your hand and close your hand into a fist to shape the rice; smooth any ridges with your fingers. The mold should be 2 inches long and 1 inch wide. Continue molding all of the Sushi "Rice" until you have 8 molds.

Place marinated shiitake caps over 4 of the sushi molds and reserve for plating.

Cut the mango slices into 2 x 1-inch rectangles and lay over the remaining rice molds.

Optional: Cut 8 very thin strips from an untoasted nori sheet. Place strips across the middle of each piece of nigiri and tuck the ends under the rice.

To make the Pickled Ginger: Place ginger, vinegar, agave nectar, and beet juice in a container with a lid. Seal container and shake to combine. Let sit for 1 to 2 hours. Can be stored for up to 1 week.

½ avocado, peeled and pitted

2 teaspoons wasabi paste

½ cup Nama Shoyu

How to Plate: Place 3 pieces of the Elephant Roll, standing up, along one side of each plate. Just before serving, cut the avocado into very thin slices and lay 1 to 2 slices over each roll. You may need to trim the avocado to fit the sushi piece perfectly.

Place 3 to 4 pieces of the Banana-Banana Roll squared off in a quarter of the plate, opposite the Elephant Rolls.

In the remaining space, artfully arrange 2 pieces of Nigiri with mushroom tops and 2 pieces with mango tops.

Place a small mound of Pickled Ginger in the corner of each serving dish. Place 1 teaspoon of wasabi paste in one corner (not pictured). Pour Nama Shoyu in two small bowls and serve on the side.

# Cashew Custard in Miso Broth

SERVES 2

## MISO BROTH

1 cup water

½ cup Nama Shoyu

2 tablespoons dried dulse

1 tablespoon dried wakame

¼ cup mellow white miso paste

## CASHEW CUSTARD

1 cup cashews, soaked in water
   1 to 2 hours

½ cup fresh young Thai coconut meat

½ cup carrageenan (see note)

¼ cup water

¼ teaspoon sea salt

## GARNISH

1 tablespoon dried wakame, soaked
   in water 2 to 3 minutes

2 (½-inch) squares untoasted nori

1 tablespoon fresh enoki mushrooms

1 teaspoon umeboshi plum paste

2 fresh cilantro leaves

To make the Miso Broth: Blend all ingredients in a blender until smooth. Store in refrigerator until ready to use.

Optional: Just before serving, place miso broth in dehydrator for 20 to 30 minutes at 105 degrees to warm.

To make the Cashew Custard: Line the bottom and sides of a small pan or square container with plastic wrap. Choose a size that will create a 1½-inch-thick custard. Drain the cashews. Blend all ingredients in a high-speed blender until completely smooth. Pour into a lined pan and cover with plastic wrap; refrigerate about 2 hours, or until firm. When ready to serve, remove custard from container by lifting plastic wrap out of pan and gently transferring custard to a cutting board.

NOTE: Raw carrageenan is a gelatinous raw red seaweed also known as Irish moss and is prepared by soaking salt-packed Irish moss until all salt is removed. Soak Irish moss overnight in cold water. Rinse thoroughly several times and blend with an equal amount of water until smooth. Store in refrigerator for up to 1 week.

How to Plate: Pour a small amount of Miso Broth in the center of shallow serving bowls or plates. Cut the Cashew Custard into 2-inch squares with a butter knife. Place 3 squares on top of the broth in each serving dish. Drain the wakame and squeeze out any extra liquid; place a small amount on top of one piece of custard. Place square of nori on top of second piece of custard and top with enoki mushrooms with stems cut short. Top the third piece with a small dollop of umeboshi plum paste and a fresh cilantro leaf. Serve immediately.

# Mochi Ice Cream

## SERVES 2

### MOCHI

1 cup cashews, soaked in water
   1 to 2 hours

¾ cup young Thai coconut meat,
   (see page 199 for instructions)

¼ cup raw agave nectar

¼ cup raw coconut oil, melted

Pinch sea salt

¼ teaspoon nonalcohol vanilla extract

Few drops nonalcohol almond extract

½ cup oat flour (see note)

¾ cup coconut flour (see note)

### GREEN TEA ICE CREAM

½ cup cashews, soaked in water
   1 to 2 hours

½ cup macadamia nuts, soaked in
   water 1 to 2 hours

½ cup young Thai coconut meat

½ cup raw agave nectar

1½ cups water

2 teaspoons nonalcohol vanilla extract

2½ tablespoons green tea powder

Pinch sea salt

½ cup coconut oil, melted

### GOJI BERRY ICE CREAM

½ cup cashews, soaked in water
   1 to 2 hours

½ cup macadamia nuts, soaked
   in water 1 to 2 hours

½ cup young Thai coconut meat

¾ cup raw agave nectar

1½ cups water

To make the Mochi: Blend cashews, coconut meat, agave nectar, coconut oil, salt, and extracts in high-speed blender until very smooth and creamy. Transfer mixture to a medium-size bowl and stir in flours until very well combined and smooth.

Line a 9 x 13-inch pan with plastic wrap on bottom and sides. Pour dough into prepared pan and spread very thin, approximately ½ inch thick. Place in freezer and freeze until firm.

NOTE: Oat flour is made by grinding whole raw oat groats in a high-speed blender or a coffee or spice grinder until a very fine flour is achieved. Coconut flour is made by grinding dried coconut flakes in the same way. Do not overprocess or the oils in the coconut will cause the coconut to cake.

To make the Green Tea, Goji Berry, and Vanilla-Lemongrass Ice Creams: For each of the three ice creams, blend all ingredients in a high-speed blender until very smooth. Pour into an ice cream maker and follow manufacturer's directions. Freeze overnight. Each ice cream recipe makes about 1 quart.

Scoop 2 large, rounded scoops of each ice cream into a pan and freeze until very firm.

2 teaspoons nonalcohol vanilla extract

1 teaspoon lemon juice

Pinch sea salt

½ cup coconut oil, melted

1 cup soaked Goji berries, soaked an
hour in warm water, blended and
strained through a fine sieve

## VANILLA-LEMONGRASS ICE CREAM

½ cup cashews, soaked in water
1 to 2 hours

½ cup macadamia nuts, soaked in
water 1 to 2 hours

½ cup young Thai coconut meat

¾ cup raw agave nectar

1½ cups water

2 teaspoons nonalcohol vanilla extract

¼ vanilla bean, scraped

¼ cup lemongrass juice (juice stalks
using the masticating-type juicers)

Pinch sea salt

½ cup coconut oil, melted

## MOCHI-COVERED ICE CREAM

Oat flour

Mochi (recipe on facing page)

## BLACK COCOA SYRUP

1½ cups raw agave nectar

½ cup cocoa powder or raw
cacao powder

2 tablespoons raw carob powder

¼ teaspoon nonalcohol vanilla extract

Pinch sea salt

½ cup coconut oil, melted

## GARNISH

Mint

Basil sprigs

To make the Mochi-Covered Ice Cream: Dust a dry cutting board with oat flour. Turn pan of frozen Mochi out onto cutting board and peel off plastic. Cut six 4 x 4-inch pieces and flatten each with floured hands until very thin. Place one scoop of the ice creams in the center of each Mochi sheet and mold Mochi around ice cream until ice cream is completely covered; smooth ridges with fingers. Place in the freezer immediately and freeze 8 to 10 hours until completely frozen.

To make the Black Cocoa Syrup: Blend all ingredients in a blender until smooth. Keep in a warm place until ready to serve.

How to Plate: Slice the ends off each Mochi-Covered Ice Cream ball to make two uniform pieces. Pour about a 2-inch-wide strip of Black Cocoa Syrup onto a dinner plate. Place a slice of each ice cream flavor partly in the syrup. Garnish with mint or basil sprigs, if desired.

# Michel Nischan

*"To cook without dairy, eggs, meat, or fish—and still get great results—requires not only skill but thoughtfulness. It's inspiring to know the days when restaurants served an uninspired plate of steamed broccoli and cherry tomatoes to vegan customers are coming to an end."*

Growing up on a farm instilled in Michel Nischan a deep appreciation for sustainable agriculture and for those who work the land. Today, as a best-selling author and chef/owner of The Dressing Room: A Homegrown Restaurant, Nischan continues to explore his love of food and the people who produce it. His son's diagnosis with juvenile diabetes began a lifelong advocacy to create a cuisine of well-being, focused on a respect for pure, local, and organic produce without the use of highly processed ingredients. Since his early days with Heartbeat at the W Hotel in New York, he has been continually lauded for his dedication to organics, sustainability, and cultural food preservation.

Nischan's interest in a more healthful, organic, and sustainable food culture introduced him to Paul Newman's daughter Nell, the driving force behind Newman's Own products. A restaurant on the grounds of the Westport Country Playhouse in Connecticut is the common home and expression of Paul Newman and Nischan's shared values of food, family, and community. A portion of The Dressing Room's proceeds supports the Westport Country Playhouse, apprenticeships for inner-city children, culinary scholarships, and community-based edible schoolyard programs.

Nischan has appeared on *ABC World News* and *Nightline,* and has won *New York Times* and James Beard Foundation book awards. He has written two books, *Homegrown Pure and Simple: Great Healthy Food From Garden to Table* and *Taste Pure and Simple: Irresistible Recipes for Good Food and Good Health.*

# Heirloom Tomato and Nectarine Salad with Full-Bodied Vinegar and Rolled Feuille de Bric

SERVES 8

6 large heirloom tomatoes

6 nectarines

1 red onion

1 cup baby arugula (optional)

2 tablespoons full-flavored vinegar
(chef suggests Banyuls made
from a wine similar to port and
aged 5 years)

6 tablespoons extra virgin olive oil

Salt and pepper to taste

ROLLED FEUILLE DE BRIC*

16 sheets phyllo dough

Soy margarine, softened

Salt and pepper

*Feuille de bric can be purchased
instead of homemade (as shown
in the photo).

Cut each tomato and nectarine into 8 wedges. Cut onion into very thin slices. If using arugula, rinse and pat dry. Whisk together vinegar and oil in a small bowl and then season with salt and pepper. Lightly toss the tomatoes, nectarines, and onions together.

To make the Rolled Feuille de Bric: Heat oven to 350 degrees F. Remove 1 sheet of phyllo dough and fold in half. Place a bowl or plate with a diameter of 6 to 8 inches across the top of the dough and with a sharp knife, cut around the rim to create two circles of dough. Brush soy margarine on the top circle from the center out. Place the top circle to the side, buttered side down. Brush soy margarine on remaining circle and the place on top of the first circle with the buttered side down. Brush the top side of the top circle with more soy margarine and sprinkle with salt and pepper. Repeat with each sheet of phyllo dough.

Using a long wooden spoon handle, carefully start at one side of the circle and roll the two circles of dough onto the handle creating a cigar-like shape. Gently slide dough off the handle and set aside while making the others, making sure to cover with plastic wrap. Place the rolls directly on the oven rack or a smaller mesh cooling rack so that they brown on all sides. Bake about 3 to 4 minutes, then turn and bake 3 to 4 minutes more. Watch carefully as times vary with each oven. Can be served immediately or stored in an airtight container.

How to Plate: Using a pastry brush, stroke vinegar and oil dressing across the plate. Artfully arrange the key ingredients partly on top of the dressing. If using arugula, it can be tossed with the other ingredients or placed on the plate to one side. Garnish with the Rolled Feuille de Bric or a favorite cracker.

# Farro Risotto with Seasonal Vegetables and Squash Blossoms

SERVES 8

## FARRO RISOTTO WITH SEASONAL VEGETABLES

2 tablespoons extra virgin olive oil

1 white onion, minced

Salt and pepper to taste

2 cups farro

4 quarts vegetable stock

½ cup wild or cultivated mushrooms, such as chanterelles and hen of the woods

½ cup each of four seasonal vegetables, such as Italian black coco beans, radishes, corn, and Roma snap beans or other mixes

Fresh herbs, such as chervil, upland cress, radish sprouts, or other mixes of thyme, parsley, marjoram, and tarragon

## FRIED SQUASH BLOSSOMS

8 to 10 large squash blossoms, or more depending on sizes

4 ounces silken tofu

4 ounces regular firm tofu

1 teaspoon orange zest

1 teaspoon fresh thyme

2 teaspoons salt, divided

Pinch of nutmeg

Canola oil

1 tablespoon flour

1 cup sparkling water

To make the Farro Risotto with Seasonal Vegetables: In a 6-quart stockpot over medium-high heat, add oil and sauté onion with a pinch of salt until translucent, about 5 to 7 minutes. Add farro and stir 1 to 2 minutes, or until farro becomes fragrant. Add 2 cups vegetable stock and continue to cook 5 minutes, stirring constantly from the bottom to prevent sticking. Add mushrooms, vegetables, salt, and another cup of vegetable stock. Cook, stirring often until the farro is al dente, about 25 minutes, adding stock as needed. Adjust seasonings and, just before serving, gently stir in herbs.

To make the Fried Squash Blossoms: Remove any remaining stems and stamens from the blossoms and check for dirt, but there's usually no need to wash. If you must wash, swish gently in cold water, shake, and drain.

In a bowl, combine tofus, zest, thyme, 1 teaspoon salt, and nutmeg. Using a pastry bag with a wide mouth (or just use a small spoon), stuff each squash blossom with the tofu mixture about two-thirds full. Twist the ends of the flowers to seal. Heat 2 inches of oil in a saucepan or skillet to 350 to 375 degrees F. Combine flour, water, and remaining salt. Coat squash blossoms with batter and slowly lower each into hot oil, frying until golden brown on each side; turn and repeat. Drain on paper towels.

How to Plate: In a shallow bowl or on a large plate, mound the Farro Risotto onto the center, garnish with additional fresh herbs, and top with one Fried Squash Blossom. Serve immediately.

# Lemon Cheesecake with Mixed Berries

SERVES 8

*Coreen Cardamone, Pastry Chef*

CRUST

2 cups crushed graham crackers

¼ cup maple syrup

¼ teaspoon almond extract

FILLING

1 pound firm or extra-firm silken tofu

⅓ cup sugar

1 tablespoon tahini, almond butter,
  or other nut butters

½ teaspoon salt

1 tablespoon lemon juice

1 teaspoon lemon zest

½ teaspoon almond extract

4 tablespoons cornstarch

2 tablespoons soy or rice milk

GARNISH

Blackberries, washed and drained

Nectarines, unpeeled, sliced, halved,
  and tossed with lemon juice to
  preserve color and add flavor

Fresh lemon juice

Mint

To make the Crust: Preheat oven to 350 degrees F. In a medium bowl, mix graham cracker crumbs, maple syrup, and almond extract until the crumbs are moistened. Press the mixture into individual oiled ramekins or other molds (4 inches diameter by 2 inches high). If you happen to have a glass slightly smaller than the ramekin, it will make a good object to press the crust into the bottom. Bake for 5 minutes. Allow the crust to cool while preparing the filling.

To make the Filling: In a food processor or blender, place tofu, sugar, tahini, salt, lemon juice, zest, and almond extract. In a small cup, stir together cornstarch and milk. Add to other ingredients. Purée until smooth and creamy, about 1 minute.

In the 350-degree F oven, pour about ⅓ cup mixture into each of eight prepared ramekins and bake about 20 minutes, or until firm. Note that the top will not rise and the cheesecakes will become firmer cooling. Cool and then refrigerate until serving.

How to Plate: Unmold cheesecakes by loosening the sides with a knife and place at one end of a long, narrow plate; garnish with blackberries and nectarines and a drizzle of lemon juice on the side. Top with a sprig of mint.

# Phil Evans

*"As a young boy I would not eat vegetables. I didn't enjoy them and found every excuse to avoid them. Now I could not be without them! Every season I can't wait for the new harvests, and every new delivery from the farmer feels like Christmas and a new toy."*

Phil Evans' culinary career includes stints at the 3-Michelin star restaurant L'Esperance in France, opening the Remington Grill at the St. Regis in Houston, then continuing with the elite hotel chain by overseeing all hotel food and beverage operations, including celebrity chef Todd English's Olives, at the St. Regis in Aspen. In 2007, Evans brought his palate to North Carolina and his passion for local seasonal ingredients, healthy spa cuisine, and wine and food pairings to Heron's at the The Umstead Hotel. Located in the Triangle region of North Carolina, the hotel is one of the country's newest privately owned and operated luxury properties.

Evans was born in upstate New York, and his interest in cooking developed early in his youth at his Italian grandmother's side. After years of cooking for his family, he attended Paul Smith's College of Arts & Sciences where he graduated at the top of his class with a degree in culinary arts. Today, his ingredient-driven menus pay tribute to the finest Southern farmers and artisans, a reminder that Heron's is sitting in the agriculturally rich triangle area of North Carolina tucked between the growing cities of Raleigh, Cary, Durham, and Chapel Hill, and the corporate world of Research Triangle Park. Heron's is poised to become a culinary beacon for local food enthusiasts, business associates seeking to impress, and destination diners in search of a superb meal and modern dining experience in the South.

# Stuffed Squash Blossoms with Mint and Fava Bean Purée

SERVES 4

## STUFFED SQUASH BLOSSOMS

8 squash blossoms

2 cups fava beans, blanched and peeled

⅓ cup mint

1 teaspoon kosher salt

Freshly ground black pepper

⅓ cup soy milk

2 tablespoons extra virgin olive oil

## MINT LIME VINAIGRETTE

5 tablespoons olive oil

2 tablespoons freshly squeezed
   lime juice

1 tablespoon minced ginger

2 tablespoons micro-diced tomato

2 tablespoons chopped fresh mint

Kosher salt and freshly ground pepper
   to taste

## CUCUMBER LIME WATER

2 English cucumbers, peeled and
   chopped

¼ cup fresh mint leaves

1 cup club soda

3 limes, juiced

2 cups crushed ice

## TEMPURA

1 cup all-purpose flour

1 cup cold water

2 tablespoons dry white wine

1 quart vegetable oil

To make the Stuffed Squash Blossoms: Clean the squash blossoms by brushing off any dirt, and then remove stems and stamen. If necessary, run a light stream of water over them and pat with a paper towel.

In a high-speed blender, combine the fava beans, mint, salt, and pepper, and process until well mixed. Add the soy milk and oil, and process until creamy. Spoon the filling into a pastry bag fitted with a large tip and pipe into the squash blossoms; refrigerate.

To make the Mint Lime Vinaigrette: In a bowl, whisk together the oil, lime juice, ginger, tomato, and mint. Season with salt and pepper; reserve.

To make the Cucumber Lime Water: Combine all the ingredients in a high-speed blender and process until smooth. Strain through a fine-mesh sieve. Pour mixture into a cocktail shaker with ice and shake vigorously; reserve.

To make the Tempura: In a large stainless steel mixing bowl, mix flour, water, and wine until smooth. In a medium saucepan, heat 4 inches oil to 340 degrees F. Dip the Stuffed Squash Blossoms in the batter and fry for 1 to 2 minutes. Drain on paper towels. Keep warm and crisp. Serve immediately.

Micro red beet tops, or other small
   greens for garnish
Micro yellow bean sprouts or other
   small greens, or mint

How to Plate: Many cooks will not have a caviar dish as shown in the photo, and a more simple way to plate is to use a dinner plate. Position the Stuffed Squash Blossom slightly off-center on a plate. Drizzle one-fourth of the Mint Lime Vinaigrette around the plate. Sprinkle some micro red beet tops, or other small greens, on top of the squash blossom. Serve with chilled Cucumber Lime Water in a glass or small bowl and top with micro yellow bean sprouts, if desired.

# Heirloom Tomatoes Three Ways

SERVES 4

### YELLOW HEIRLOOM TOMATO WATER WITH MICRO FENNEL

6 yellow heirloom tomatoes, washed and cores removed

¾ cup fennel fronds

3 tablespoons granulated sugar

1 tablespoon kosher salt

Baby fennel root, shaved

Tomato powder, bought or homemade

10 Roma tomatoes, if making tomato powder (see note)

### HEIRLOOM TOMATO SALAD

3 Cherokee purple tomatoes, washed and cores removed

1 small red onion, peeled and finely julienned

1 tablespoon sugar

Kosher salt and freshly ground white pepper to taste

3 tablespoons white balsamic vinegar

¼ cup extra virgin olive oil

¼ cup micro cutting celery, parsley, or other micro greens

### HEIRLOOM TOMATO CARPACCIO WITH GREY SALT

2 black brandy wine heirloom tomatoes, washed and cores removed

2 tablespoons cold-pressed extra virgin olive oil

1 teaspoon grey salt (moist unrefined sea salt)

¼ cup micro fennel

To make the Yellow Heirloom Tomato Water with Micro Fennel: Combine all ingredients in a high-speed blender and process until smooth. Pour mixture into a fine mesh sieve lined with two layers of cheesecloth. Tie cheesecloth tightly into a bundle with butcher's twine and hang over a bowl in the refrigerator for 24 hours. (Twine must be tight enough to add pressure to assist with draining.)

NOTE: For homemade tomato powder, blanch the Roma tomatoes, put in an ice bath to cool, and pull off skins. Using a dehydrator, dehydrate to completely dry, or heat for about 2 hours in a 200-degree F oven after placing the skins on a nonstick surface. Cool and grind into a powder in a coffee grinder, high-speed blender, or food processor.

Pour into a small glass bowl and serve chilled. Garnish with shaved fennel and tomato powder.

To make the Heirloom Tomato Salad: Slice tomatoes into quarters and toss in a mixing bowl with onion, sugar, salt, pepper, vinegar, and oil. Marinate for 5 to 10 minutes before serving. Evenly divide tomato pieces among four very small bowls, perhaps 3 inches in diameter, and garnish with the cutting celery, parsley, or other micro greens.

To make the Heirloom Tomato Carpaccio with Grey Salt: Slice tomatoes very thin and shingle 4 to 5 slices on a plate. Drizzle with oil and grey salt; top with micro fennel.

How to Plate: If a long narrow plate is available, place each recipe in a row on the plate. Otherwise, a large square plate can be used and artfully arrange the three recipes in a triangle. Drizzle some olive oil on the plate to garnish, if desired.

# Baby Squash, Morels, and Cauliflower with Rhubarb and Beet Broth

SERVES 4

## RHUBARB AND BEET BROTH

8 cups water

2 cups chopped rhubarb

2 cups peeled and chopped red beets

1 tablespoon fresh thyme

1 fresh bay leaf

1 tablespoon white peppercorns

1 tablespoon kosher salt

## SAUTÉED BABY SQUASH, MORELS, AND CAULIFLOWER

¼ cup sliced baby zucchini

¼ cup sliced baby yellow squash

½ cup quartered sunburst squash

½ cup cauliflower florets

¼ cup fresh English peas

¼ cup asparagus tips

¼ cup carmellini beans or haricot verts

16 small white pearl onions, peeled

1 shallot, finely minced

2 tablespoons grapeseed oil

½ cup halved morel mushrooms

¼ cup dry white wine

1 tablespoon fresh thyme

Kosher salt and fresh ground white
    pepper to taste

## ASPARAGUS SALAD

12 pieces jumbo asparagus

2 teaspoons champagne vinegar

1 tablespoon extra virgin olive oil,
    plus more to garnish

To make the Rhubarb and Beet Broth: In a medium saucepan, combine water, rhubarb, beets, thyme, bay leaf, peppercorns, and salt and bring to a boil. Reduce heat and simmer for 1 hour. Strain through a fine mesh sieve; return liquid to heat and simmer for approximately 15 minutes, or until reduced to 3 cups.

To make the Sautéed Baby Squash, Morels, and Cauliflower: In a small saucepan, blanch zucchini, squash, cauliflower, peas, asparagus, beans, and onions separately until tender. Shock in an ice water bath and then drain and set aside.

In a large sauté pan over medium heat, lightly caramelize shallot in oil. Add mushrooms, sauté for 1 to 2 minutes, and then add the blanched vegetables. Continue cooking for 1 to 2 minutes, or until lightly caramelized. Deglaze pan with wine; season with thyme, salt, and pepper. Keep warm until plating.

To make the Asparagus Salad: Using a mandolin, julienne the asparagus lengthwise to obtain long thin strips. Toss asparagus, vinegar, and oil and reserve until ready for plating.

How to Plate: Arrange the Sautéed Baby Squash, Morels, and Cauliflower in four individual bowls. Spoon in Rhubarb and Beet Broth, and then drizzle with oil. Top with the Asparagus Salad and a variety of edible flowers.

# Mango-Spearmint, Raspberry-Rosemary, and Lemon-Thyme Sorbets with Mango-Spearmint, Raspberry-Rosemary, and Lemon-Thyme Waters

## MANGO-SPEARMINT SORBET

3 cups peeled and chopped
   ripe mango
¼ cup freshly squeezed lemon juice
½ cup water
⅓ cup simple syrup
2 tablespoons chopped fresh
   spearmint

## MANGO-SPEARMINT WATER

1 mango, peeled and chopped
2 navel oranges, juiced
1 tablespoon chopped fresh spearmint
2 tablespoons simple syrup
½ cup filtered water
1½ cups crushed ice

## RASPBERRY-ROSEMARY SORBET

3 cups fresh raspberries
¼ cup freshly squeezed lime juice
½ cup water
⅓ cup simple syrup
1 teaspoon fresh rosemary

## RASPBERRY-ROSEMARY WATER

2 cups raspberries
1 lime, juiced
¼ teaspoon fresh rosemary
2 tablespoons simple syrup
½ cup filtered water
1½ cups crushed ice

NOTE: Each sorbet makes about 1 quart, more than is needed for this recipe. If making all three sorbets, consider making 1 cup of simple syrup in advance and dividing it as the recipes require.

NOTE: To make the simple syrup to use in the sorbets, heat 2 cups sugar and 1 cup water together in a saucepan. Bring to a boil until sugar is dissolved and reduce heat until the mixture is a syrupy consistency. Cool slightly, or store in a refrigerator until ready to use.

To make the Mango-Spearmint Sorbet: Combine all ingredients in a blender and purée for 3 minutes, or until smooth. Strain through a fine mesh sieve and refrigerate for 1 hour to chill. Freeze in an ice cream maker according to the manufacturer's directions. Spread sorbet into an 8 x 8-inch pan resulting in an inch depth of sorbet.

To make the Mango-Spearmint Water: If selected fruit is especially sweet, adjust the amount of simple syrup accordingly. Combine all ingredients except ice in a high-speed blender and process until smooth. Strain through a fine mesh sieve. Pour into a cocktail shaker with ice; shake well and pour into small juice glasses.

To make the Raspberry-Rosemary Sorbet: Combine all ingredients in a blender and purée for 3 minutes, or until smooth. Strain through a fine mesh sieve and refrigerate for 1 hour to chill. Freeze in an ice cream maker according to the manufacturer's directions. Spread sorbet into an 8 x 8-inch pan resulting in an inch depth of sorbet..

To make the Raspberry-Rosemary Water: If selected fruit is especially sweet, adjust the amount of simple syrup accordingly. Combine all ingredients except ice in a high-speed blender and process until smooth. Strain through a fine mesh sieve. Pour into a cocktail shaker with ice; shake well and pour into small juice glasses.

## LEMON-THYME SORBET

3 cups freshly squeezed lemon juice
¼ cup freshly squeezed lime juice
½ cup water
⅓ cup simple syrup
2 tablespoons fresh thyme

## LEMON-THYME WATER

2 cups freshly squeezed lemon juice
1 tablespoon fresh thyme
2 tablespoons simple syrup
1 cup club soda
1½ cups crushed ice

## GARNISH

Fresh micro herbs
Lemon zest

To make the Lemon-Thyme Sorbet: Combine all ingredients in a blender and purée for 3 minutes, or until smooth. Strain through a fine mesh sieve and refrigerate for 1 hour to chill. Freeze in an ice cream maker according to the manufacturer's directions. Spread sorbet into an 8 x 8-inch pan resulting in an inch depth of sorbet.

To make the Lemon-Thyme Water: Combine all ingredients in a cocktail shaker; shake well and pour into small juice glasses.

How to Plate: Once ready for assembly, remove sorbets from freezer. Cut each sorbet into 2-inch long slices, creating pieces that measure 1 x 1 x 2-inches. Place one of each sorbet on a plate. If the plate is long and narrow, place the sorbets in a row and place each flavored water with respective sorbets. Garnish with fresh micro herbs of choice. Lemon zest can also serve as a garnish, if desired.

# Suzanne Goin

*"Thoughtful seasoning is the key to great-tasting food."*

Before Suzanne Goin graduated from Brown University with honors, she had already distinguished herself with multiple courses in the celebrated kitchens of Ma Maison, L'Orangerie, Al Forno, and La Magarin. Following a culinary passion inspired by francophilic parents, she worked with Alice Waters at Chez Panisse in Berkeley and subsequently with Michelin-star luminaries Didier Oudill and Alain Pasard in France. Her return to the United States in 1993 included stints at Olives and Alloro in Boston and at David Peel's celebrated La Campanile in Los Angeles.

In 1998, she opened Lucques, and within the year she was hailed as one of the country's Best New Chefs by *Food & Wine* magazine. With her business partner, Caroline Styne, she opened A.O.C. in 2002, and in 2005, with husband and fellow chef, David Lentz, The Hungry Cat, a casual Hollywood eatery, made its debut. Goin has garnered national recognition in the *New York Times, Bon Appétit, Wine Spectator, Los Angeles* magazine, the *Los Angeles Times, Vogue,* and *Town and Country.* Her cookbook *Sunday Suppers at Lucques* is in its second printing. In 2006, it won a James Beard Foundation cookbook award and she was also named Best Chef: California.

# Succotash Salad

1 tablespoon finely diced shallot

3 tablespoons lemon juice, plus
  more to taste

Salt

½ cup plus 2 tablespoons extra
  virgin olive oil

¾ cup diced red onion

2 teaspoons thyme leaves

2 cups diced summer squash

3 cups fresh corn (about 4 ears)

¼ teaspoon pepper

½ pint cherry tomatoes, cut in half

1 cup cooked fresh lima beans,
  well drained

¼ cup chiffonade basil, opal and
  green mix

1 tablespoon sliced parsley

1 tablespoon minced chives

4 ounces mixed salad of arugula
  and watercress

Place shallot, 3 tablespoons lemon juice, and ½ teaspoon salt in a bowl and let sit for 5 minutes. Whisk in 5 tablespoons oil and then taste for balance and seasoning.

Heat a large sauté pan over high heat for 2 minutes. Add 3 tablespoons oil, onion, and thyme; sauté about 1 minute. Add squash and season with 1 teaspoon salt. Cook another 4 minutes, or until tender and it has a little color; set aside to cool.

Wipe out the pan with paper towels and return it to the stove. Heat on high for about 2 minutes. Add the remaining 2 tablespoons oil, corn, 1 teaspoon salt, and ¼ teaspoon pepper. Sauté for about 2 minutes, tossing often, until the corn is just tender; set aside to cool.

Place the tomatoes in a large salad bowl and season with ½ teaspoon salt. Add the squash, corn, and lima beans. Toss with half the dressing. Taste for seasoning and adjust with more salt and lemon juice if desired. Gently toss the herbs into the succotash. Toss the arugula and watercress with the remaining dressing, and then season with a pinch of salt and pepper.

How to Plate: Place the arugula and watercress salad on a large chilled platter and arrange the succotash over top.

# Yellow Tomato Gazpacho

SERVES 6

2½ pounds ripe yellow tomatoes

3 Persian cucumbers or 1 hothouse
   English cucumber

½ jalapeño, seeded and cut in half

4 sprigs cilantro plus 12 cilantro
   leaves

2 cloves garlic, coarsely chopped

2 tablespoons red wine vinegar

⅓ cup extra virgin olive oil, plus more

1 tablespoon salt

Black pepper to taste

3 tablespoons diced red or orange
   sweet bell pepper

3 tablespoons diced red onion

18 small cherry tomatoes, cut in half

Kosher salt and freshly ground black
   pepper to taste

Olive oil

Blanch the yellow tomatoes in boiling water for 30 seconds and then shock in a bowl of ice water for a few minutes to cool; reserve the ice water. Use your fingers to remove the skins. Remove the cores and chop tomatoes coarsely, saving all the juice. Seed and dice 3 tablespoons of unpeeled cucumber as neatly as possible for the garnish; set aside. Peel the remaining cucumber and coarsely chop. The soup will need to be made in two batches. Place half of each of the chopped tomatoes, cucumbers, jalapeño, cilantro, garlic, vinegar, and oil in a blender with 1 tablespoon salt and some pepper. Process in a blender on the lowest speed until broken down. Turn speed up to high and purée until the soup is completely smooth. Use the reserved ice water to thin the soup if it is too thick. Pour the soup through a strainer and taste for seasoning; repeat with the remaining ingredients. Chill the soup in the refrigerator; it should be served very cold.

How to Plate: Combine bell pepper, onion, and reserved diced cucumber together in a small bowl. Pour the gazpacho into chilled soup bowls and scatter the pepper mixture over the soup. Season cherry tomatoes with salt and pepper and place 3 tomato halves and 2 cilantro leaves at the center of each bowl. Finish with a drizzle of oil.

# *Grilled Polenta with Fresh Shell Bean Ragout*

SERVES 4

## GRILLED POLENTA

5½ cups water

1 tablespoon salt

1 cup medium-grain polenta (chef
prefers Bob's Red Mill)

2 tablespoons olive oil, plus more

## FRESH SHELL BEAN RAGOUT

8 tablespoons olive oil, divided

¼ cup finely diced onion

2 teaspoons minced garlic

2 teaspoons thyme leaves

3 cups fresh shell beans (at least
2 types such as flagolets, black
beans, black-eyed peas, limas,
or cranberry beans)

Kosher salt to taste

½ pound haricots verts, stems
removed, tails left on

2 tablespoons finely diced shallot

2 tablespoons sliced opal basil

2 tablespoons chopped flat-leaf
parsley

To make the Grilled Polenta: In a heavy-bottomed saucepan, bring water and salt to a boil over high heat. Add polenta slowly, whisking continuously. Turn heat down to low and continue cooking for another 20 minutes, whisking often. Add another ½ cup water as needed, about every 20 minutes to keep smooth and moist. The heat should be low so that the polenta is barely simmering. As you whisk, make sure you reach the bottom of the pan to prevent the polenta from scorching. For the purposes of grilling, the polenta should be a little thicker than it would be if you were serving it soft.

Whisk in 2 tablespoons oil and taste for seasoning. Pour the polenta onto a lightly oiled baking sheet—it should be about ³/₄ inch thick. Chill overnight and then cut polenta into triangles.

Light the grill 30 to 40 minutes before cooking. When the coals are broken down, red, and glowing, brush both sides of the polenta with oil and grill the triangles for 5 to 6 minutes, until you have nice marks. Turn the polenta over and cook until you have nice color on the second side and the polenta is very hot.

To make the Fresh Shell Bean Ragout: For each type of bean, heat a medium saucepan over medium heat for 2 minutes. Swirl 2 tablespoons oil into each pan and divide onion, garlic, and thyme between them. Sauté over medium heat about 5 minutes, or until the onion is translucent. Add the shell beans (again, cooking each variety separately), and cook for a few minutes, stirring to coat them in the oil. Add salt and water to cover 2 inches. Simmer 10 to 15 minutes, or until the beans are just tender. (Cooking time will vary depending on the types of beans used. Taste to see if they are done.) Remove from the heat and then cool the beans in the cooking liquid.

While the beans are cooking, blanch haricots verts in a large pot of salted boiling water for 2 to 3 minutes until tender but still al dente. Transfer the haricots verts onto a baking sheet to cool.

## CHERRY TOMATO–OLIVE SAUCE

Olive oil

1 cup halved cherry tomatoes

Kosher salt and pepper to taste

2 tablespoons diced shallot

3 tablespoons sliced black olives

½ lemon, for juicing

1 tablespoon parsley

2 tablespoons sliced basil, both green and purple (if possible)

Drain the shell beans, reserving the cooking liquid. Heat a large sauté pan over high heat for 1 minute. Swirl in remaining oil, add haricots verts, and shallot to the pan. Add the shell beans, and stir gently, being careful not to crush the beans. Add about ½ cup shell bean cooking liquid to the pan to moisten the ragout. Taste for seasoning and cook a few minutes until beans are hot. Add opal basil and parsley right before serving.

To make the Cherry Tomato–Olive Sauce: Heat oil in a medium sauté pan over medium high heat for 1 minute. Add tomatoes and season with salt and pepper. Let the tomatoes pop and sizzle in the pan. Add shallot and black olives; toss to combine. Season to taste with lemon juice, and add parsley and basil at the last minute.

How to Plate: Arrange the Fresh Shell Bean Ragout on the bottom of a shallow bowl or plate. Top with the Grilled Polenta and spoon Cherry Tomato–Olive Sauce over and around the beans and the polenta. Finish with a few sprigs of flat-leaf parsley.

# Terrance Brennan

*"To me, the vegan lifestyle focuses on clean and healthy flavors, the purity of seasonal ingredients, and eating for the mind, body, and soul. Participating in this book was a natural extension of my own food philosophy, because every day I look to local produce as the starting point to building any dish."*

Terrance Brennan is the chef-proprietor of Picholine Restaurant and Artisanal Bistro and Wine Bar, two highly acclaimed restaurants in New York City, and the founder of Artisanal Premium Cheese, a wholesale and online gourmet cheese company and education center. The son of Annandale, Virginia, restaurateurs, Brennan began cooking at the age of thirteen. In the south of France, his French-Mediterranean cuisine was inspired by Roger Verge at Moulin de Mougins and working in kitchens that included Le Cirque, Taillevent, Le Tour D'Argent, Gualtiero Marchesi, and Gavroche. In 1993, Brennan opened his first restaurant, naming it Picholine after the petite green olives on the Mediterranean coast.

Picholine received a James Beard Foundation nomination for the country's Outstanding Restaurant in 2007, and was awarded two stars in the 2008 edition of Michelin Guide: New York City. It has earned two three-star reviews from the *New York Times* and has received Zagat's Highest Overall ratings since 1997.

Brennan extended its groundbreaking cheese service with Artisinal, a bistro–wine bar–fromagerie voted Best Brasserie Cuisine in the 2002 Zagat Survey and one of New York's most popular restaurants. In 2007, Brennan set the Guinness World Record for the World's Largest Fondue live on NBC's *Today Show* and has also appeared on the Food Network and the *Martha Stewart Show.*

Named a Best New Chef by *Food & Wine* magazine in 1995, Brennan is a four-time nominee for Best Chef: New York by the James Beard Foundation. His first cookbook, *Artisanal Cooking: A Chef Shares His Passion for Handcrafting Great Meals at Home,* was published in 2005.

# *White Gazpacho with Red Gazpacho Granité*

SERVES 6

### WHITE GAZPACHO

2 cups plus 3 tablespoons peeled,
    thinly sliced almonds

1 cup seedless green grapes

¾ cup cucumber juice, extracted
    from peeled cucumbers in a juicer
    or purchased from a juice bar

¼ cup verjus or 2 tablespoons
    sherry vinegar

To make the White Gazpacho: In batches, put 2 cups almonds, grapes, cucumber juice, verjus, oil, vinegar, and garlic into a blender. Pour in 3 cups of water and blend until uniformly smooth, approximately 4 minutes. Add the bread and process for 1 minute more. Taste, season with the salt and cayenne, taste again, and add more salt if necessary. Cover, and refrigerate for at least 3 hours or up to 24 hours. If it appears too thick after refrigeration, whisk in some cold water to thin.

1 cup fruity extra virgin olive oil

2 tablespoons plus 2 teaspoons
  sherry vinegar

2 small cloves garlic, peeled

3 cups water

1 cup small, crustless white bread
  cubes (from 1½ ounces or 2 to
  3 slices bread)

1 tablespoon kosher salt

½ teaspoon cayenne

### RED GAZPACHO GRANITÉ

1 pound fresh beefsteak tomatoes,
  cored and passed through a food mill
  (about 1½ cups milled tomatoes)

2 tablespoons cucumber juice,
  extracted from peeled cucumbers in
  a juicer or purchased from a juice bar

1 tablespoon red pepper juice,
  extracted in a juicer or purchased in
  a juice bar

2 teaspoons celery juice, extracted in
  a juicer or purchased in a juice bar

1 tablespoon sherry vinegar

1 teaspoon finely chopped garlic

Kosher salt to taste

Pinch cayenne pepper, or more to taste

### GARNISH

1 tablespoon finely diced red bell
  pepper (optional)

1 tablespoon finely diced, peeled,
  and seeded cucumber (optional)

1 tablespoon finely diced red onion
  (optional)

1 tablespoon finely diced celery
  (optional)

30 cilantro leaves

When ready to serve, put the remaining almonds in an 8-inch sauté pan and toast over medium heat, shaking constantly, until fragrant, about 1 to 2 minutes. Transfer to a small bowl and cool to room temperature. If using all or some of the Garnish (see below), add and stir gently but thoroughly; reserve.

NOTE: Verjus is a non-fermented juice from unripe green grapes with high acidity and a tart apple-like flavor, and is a wine-friendly alternative to vinegar.

To make the Red Gazpacho Granité: Put all ingredients except the salt and cayenne in a mixing bowl and stir together. Season with salt and cayenne, or more for a spicier granité. Pour the mixture into a 9 x 9-inch Pyrex dish and put in the freezer. Freeze for at least 2 hours, or until frozen, scraping the mixture with a fork every half-hour to break it into crystals. The granité can be covered and frozen for up to 1 week. When ready to serve, scoop out portions with an ice-cream scoop.

How to Plate: Put a ¼-cup scoop of Red Gazpacho Granité in the center of each bowl. Place garnishes in a ring around the granité. Divide and gently pour the gazpacho in the bowls. Arrange 5 cilantro leaves decoratively on top of each.

# Warm Provençal Vegetables with Olives and Basil Tempura

SERVES 6

## PROVENÇAL VEGETABLES

5 tablespoons extra virgin olive oil

2 cloves garlic, minced

2 teaspoons chopped fresh thyme

½ pound zucchini, cut diagonally into ¼-inch-thick pieces

½ pound yellow squash, cut diagonally into ¼-inch-thick pieces

½ pound Japanese or regular eggplant, cut diagonally into ¼-inch-thick pieces

1 red pepper, roasted and then sliced into ¼-inch pieces

½ pound baby fennel, cleaned, or 1 medium bulb, cleaned and cut into 8 lengthwise pieces

1 teaspoon salt

Freshly ground black pepper

## BASIL TEMPURA

5 tablespoons all-purpose flour

3 tablespoons cornstarch

½ teaspoon baking powder

½ teaspoon fine sea salt

½ cup soda water

30 basil leaves, washed and patted dry

## NIÇOISE OLIVE TAPENADE

1 cup niçoise olives

1 teaspoon lemon juice

⅛ teaspoon sherry vinegar

1 tablespoon capers

⅛ teaspoon minced garlic

⅓ cup extra virgin olive oil

To make the Provençal Vegetables: Combine the oil, garlic, and thyme in a large bowl. Add the vegetables and toss thoroughly until evenly coated. Marinate for 30 minutes and then season with salt and freshly ground pepper. Preheat an outdoor grill or grill pan over medium heat. Grill the vegetables until they are lightly charred and tender, about 3 minutes per side; set aside.

To make the Basil Tempura: Preheat a deep fryer to 325 degrees F. In a small mixing bowl, sift the flour, cornstarch, baking powder, and sea salt. With a fork, gently stir in the soda water. With a 2-inch pastry brush, brush the basil leaves on both sides with a generous layer of the batter. Deep-fry until crisp, about 1 minute. Using a slotted spoon, transfer to a paper towel–lined plate to drain; set aside.

To make the Niçoise Olive Tapenade: In a food processor, blend the ingredients until coarse, about 1 minute; set aside.

How to Plate: Arrange the Provençal Vegetables artfully between six plates. Drizzle the Niçoise Olive Tapenade evenly over the vegetables and place 5 pieces of Basil Tempura on top of each plate. Serve immediately.

# Risotto with Cauliflower and Black Truffle Gremoulata

## SERVES 6

### TRUFFLE GREMOULATA

½ cup ground white bread (dried and
   ground in a food processor)
¼ cup chopped black truffles
   (if unavailable, use portobello
   mushrooms)
1 teaspoon chopped parsley
Zest of 1 lemon
¼ teaspoon chopped garlic
¼ teaspoon salt

### ROASTED CAULIFLOWER

1 tablespoon extra virgin olive oil
½ pound cauliflower florets, sliced
   ¼ inch thick
Salt to taste

### CAULIFLOWER PURÉE

3 cups water
1 teaspoon salt
½ pound cauliflower florets, cut
   into small pieces

### RISOTTO

4 tablespoons extra virgin olive oil
¼ cup diced white onion
¼ teaspoon salt
½ teaspoon minced garlic
2 cups carnaroli or other risotto rice
   such as Arborio or vialone nano
½ cup dry white wine
4 cups hot vegetable stock

To make the Truffle Gremoulata: In a medium bowl, combine all the ingredients; set aside.

To make the Roasted Cauliflower: Preheat the broiler. In a large bowl, toss the oil with the cauliflower and season well with salt. Place the cauliflower in a single layer on a baking sheet. Cook under the broiler until golden brown and tender, about 3 minutes; set aside.

To make the Cauliflower Purée: Bring the water to a boil over medium heat in a 2-quart saucepan. Add the salt and cauliflower, and simmer until tender, about 10 minutes. Drain cauliflower in a colander and purée in a blender until smooth; set aside.

To make the Risotto: Heat the oil in a 4-quart saucepan over medium-low heat. Add the onion and salt, and cook until softened but not browned, about 4 minutes. Add the garlic and sauté for 1 minute. Add carnaroli and stir to coat, about 1 minute. Add the white wine and continue to stir. Once the wine has been absorbed by the rice, add 1 cup of the vegetable stock, stirring constantly. Once the stock has been absorbed by the rice, add another cup. Repeat the process with the remaining stock, stirring constantly. After adding about half the stock, vigorously stir and agitate the rice for 30 seconds to release its starch content. When finished, the rice should be very thick and creamy, and should hold its shape for a moment when stirred before falling slightly.

How to Plate: Fold the Cauliflower Purée into the Risotto. Divide evenly among six plates or shallow bowls. Arrange the Roasted Cauliflower evenly on top and then top with the Truffle Gremoulata. Garnish with more truffle slices and parsley leaves. Serve immediately.

# Pear "Belle Helen" Chocolate Soup and Cinnamon Croutons

SERVES 6

## PEARS

2 cups water

2 cups dry white wine

1 cup sugar

1 cinnamon stick

3 ripe Bartlett pears, peeled and
   halved lengthwise

## CHOCOLATE SOUP

2 cups water

½ cup sugar

3 tablespoons cocoa powder

½ cup chopped bittersweet chocolate

## CINNAMON CROUTONS

2 tablespoons hazelnut oil

1 cup (¼-inch) cubed country bread
   or baguette, with the crust

½ teaspoon ground cinnamon

5 teaspoons sugar

## VANILLA SOY GELATO

8 ounces soy yogurt

2 cups soy milk

⅓ cup maple syrup

2 teaspoons vanilla

**To make the Pears:** In a 2-quart saucepan bring the water, wine, sugar, and cinnamon stick to a simmer. Add the pear halves and continue to simmer until tender, about 10 minutes. Remove from heat and let cool. Using a melon baller, scoop out the center core and the seeds, and discard. Transfer mixture to a large bowl, cover, and refrigerate for at least 3 hours.

**To make the Chocolate Soup:** Combine the water, sugar, and cocoa powder in a 2-quart saucepan and bring to a simmer, whisking often. Place the chocolate in a small mixing bowl and add the hot mixture; whisk until smooth.

**To make the Cinnamon Croutons:** Warm the hazelnut oil in a heavy-bottomed saucepan over low heat. Add the bread cubes and toast in the oil until golden brown, about 3 minutes. Place the toasted bread cubes in a small bowl. Add the cinnamon and sugar and toss to coat; set aside.

**To make the Vanilla Soy Gelato:** In a large mixing bowl, combine all ingredients. Transfer mixture to an ice cream maker and freeze according to manufacturer's directions.

**How to Plate:** Divide pear halves evenly among six bowls. Top with a scoop of Vanilla Soy Gelato. Place Cinnamon Croutons on top and along the sides. Carefully pour about ¾ cup Chocolate Soup into the bottom of each the bowl. Serve immediately.

# Thomas Keller

*"Food has to touch the soul."*

Thomas Keller is one of the most inventive and respected chefs working in the United States today. In 2001, he was named America's Best Chef by *Time* magazine and World Master of Culinary Arts at the Wedgewood Awards. He was the recipient of the Lifetime Achievement Award from the Food Allergy Initiative and has collected numerous other accolades in the past decade, including consecutive Best Chef awards from the James Beard Foundation—the first chef ever to achieve this honor.

In 1994, he opened The French Laundry in Napa, California, and in 2003, it was rated at the top of the World's Best 50 Restaurants in London's Restaurant magazine. His bistro, Couchon opened in 1998 with Bouchon Bakery five years later. In 2004, Per Se in New York received a four-star rating in the *New York Times* and was also heralded in *Gourmet, Food & Wine,* and *New York Magazine,* and rated Best New Restaurant of the Year by *Restaurant* magazine. Keller owns eight properties in the United States. In addition to The French Laundry, Per Se and Bouchon, branches of Bouchon and Bouchon Bakery opened in Las Vegas. Soon afterward, Bouchon Bakery opened at Time Warner Center in New York City. Most recently, Ad Hoc, a casual dining establishment inspired by the comfort food he enjoyed growing up, opened in Yountville, California.

The prestigious Michelin Guide recently gave both The French Laundry and PerSe a three-star rating, making Thomas Keller the only American-born chef to hold multiple three-star ratings.

# Purée of Sunchoke Soup with Pickled Red Radishes and Country Bread Croutons

SERVES 4

2 bunches red radishes, cleaned
  and trimmed

2½ cups water, divided

1 cup champagne vinegar

1 cup plus 1 teaspoon sugar, divided

4 slices country bread

¾ cup extra virgin olive oil, divided

2 ounces yellow onions

1 tablespoon kosher salt

4 cups vegetable stock

14 ounces sunchokes

## GARNISH
Micro greens

Place radishes in a medium glass bowl. Bring 2 cups water and vinegar to a boil in a small pot. Dissolve 1 cup sugar in liquid and pour over radishes. Allow to cool at room temperature and strain; slice to desired shape.

Slice the bread into small cubes. Sauté in ½ cup oil until golden brown. Season with a pinch of salt and drain well on paper towels.

Sweat onions in remaining oil until completely soft. Add remaining sugar, salt, vegetable stock, and sunchokes. Cook over medium heat until sunchokes are completely soft. At this point, the stock should be reduced by half. Add remaining water, bring to a boil, and taste for salt. Transfer soup to a blender. Purée soup in blender and pass through a fine mesh sieve.

How to Plate: Place a small pile of pickled radishes and croutons in the middle of a soup bowl. Carefully pour soup into warm bowls. Garnish with micro greens.

# Salad of Roasted Baby Beets, Cipollini Onions, with Shaved Black Truffle, and Sauce Soubise

SERVES 4

## ROASTED BEETS

8 baby red beets, about ¾ inch in diameter

8 baby yellow beets, about ¾ inch in diameter

3 tablespoons extra virgin olive oil

4 tablespoons sugar, divided

2 tablespoons kosher salt

## CIPOLLINI ONIONS

12 whole cipollini onions, peeled

2 tablespoons salt, divided

2 tablespoons sugar, divided

1 tablespoon champagne vinegar

1 tablespoon extra virgin olive oil

## BLACK TRUFFLE

1 black truffle

Fleur de sel

Champagne vinegar

Extra-virgin olive oil

## SAUCE SOUBISE

2 Spanish onions, peeled and cut in half

1 tablespoon canola oil

2 tablespoons sugar

2 tablespoons salt

2 tablespoons steamed white rice

To make the Roasted Beets: Wash and trim the beets, keeping the colors separate. Put half of the oil, sugar, and salt in each of two mixing bowls; add red beets to one bowl and yellow to the other. Wrap the beets, keeping the colors separate, in aluminum foil, sealing tight. Bake at 375 degrees F for 45 minutes, or until tender. Remove from oven and let cool to room temperature. Once completely cooled, save beet juice to use for garnish. Peel skin off the beets and cut into quarters.

To make the Cipollini Onions: Place onions in a small pot and cover twice over with cold water. Add 1 tablespoon each of salt and sugar. Slowly bring mixture to a simmer over low heat. Let simmer for 10 minutes, or until onions are soft. Drain the water and set onions aside to cool. Heat a small sauté pan and oil lightly. Quickly sauté cooked onions; gently turn over when lightly caramelized. Combine the remaining salt and sugar, champagne vinegar, and oil in a bowl, and lightly toss the onions with the mixture; set aside.

To make the Black Truffle: Shave truffle very thinly using a truffle slicer or mandolin. Season to taste with fleur de sel, vinegar, and oil; set aside.

To make the Sauce Soubise: Cut onions into ¼-inch slices; place in a medium saucepot and cover with cold water. Bring to a boil over high heat and then strain water from pot. Incorporate oil with onions over medium heat. Add sugar and salt, and sweat until fully cooked, adding water if necessary. Place cooked onions in a blender and purée. Add rice to achieve proper sauce consistency and purée until smooth. Taste and season if needed. Strain through a fine mesh sieve and chill.

## GARNISH
Beet sprouts and other available shoots

**How to Plate:** Using a pastry brush, spread reserved beet juices onto a plate. Spoon Sauce Soubise around the plate and place the Roasted Beets on top, alternating colors. Place Cipollini Onions and Black Truffle slices along each side of the beets. Garnish with beet sprouts and other available shoots.

# Salad of Riesling-Poached Tokyo Turnips with Brussels Sprouts, Pickled French Laundry Garden Onions, and Toasted Mustard Seed Emulsion

SERVES 6

2 large Spanish onions, thinly sliced

3½ tablespoons Dijon mustard

⅔ cup vegetable oil

¾ tablespoon mustard seeds, toasted
   and blanched until tender

2 cups Riesling (preferably Gunderloch
   "Nackenheimer Rothenberg"
   Auslese, Rheingau, 2004)

18 small Tokyo turnips

¼ cup plus 3 tablespoons sugar

⅛ teaspoon kosher salt, plus more
   to adjust seasoning

18 small Brussels sprouts

6 Vidalia onion shoots

6 small red pearl onions

¾ tablespoon champagne vinegar

GARNISH

Chives, cut into 1-inch pieces, some
   split and curled

Mustard powder*


*Made from grinding 1 tablespoon each
   of black and yellow mustard seeds
   to a fine powder in a coffee or spice
   grinder, then sifting through a fine
   mesh strainer

Wrap the Spanish onions in aluminum foil with ¼ cup sugar and bake in a 350-degree F oven until completely tender, about 1 to 1½ hours. Empty the onions into a fine mesh sieve and press them with a spoon to extract as much liquid as possible into a bowl. Combine onion liquid with the Dijon mustard and slowly whisk in the oil. Season with mustard seeds and salt.

Reduce wine by half in a medium saucepot over medium heat. Add turnips, 1½ tablespoons sugar, and salt; reduce until dry. Turnips should be tender. Do not caramelize the remaining syrup. If needed, add a touch of water to finish cooking and reduce until dry. Remove from pan and reserve for later use.

Blanch the Brussels sprouts and onion shoots separately. Bring a large pot of heavily salted water to a rolling boil (larger than what would seem to be necessary in order to protect the color of the Brussels sprouts). Put Brussels sprouts in pot and cook until fork tender. Remove sprouts and place directly into an ice water bath. Cool completely in ice bath, remove, and reserve for later use. Repeat the same process with the onion shoots.

Place pearl onions in a small pot with 1½ tablespoons sugar and vinegar. Fill with enough water to cover. Reduce over medium heat until all the water has evaporated. Be careful not to caramelize the remaining sugar and vinegar syrup. Onions should be completely tender. Remove from pan and reserve for later use.

How to Plate: Combine vegetables and dress lightly with the mustard emulsion. Arrange 3 Brussels sprouts (each cut in various ways—whole, half, quarter) and 1 red pearl onion, halved, on each plate. Add turnips and an onion shoot. Dot mustard emulsion around the vegetables. Garnish with chives and dust with mustard powder.

# Caramelized Bananas and Bitter Chocolate Cake with Coconut and Chocolate Sorbet and Chocolate Sauce

SERVES 8

*Sebastien Rouxel, Pastry Chef*

### BITTER CHOCOLATE CAKE

1½ cups all-purpose flour

1 cup castor sugar

3 tablespoons cocoa powder

1 teaspoon baking soda

½ teaspoon salt

1 tablespoon vinegar

1 cup water

¼ cup plus 1 tablespoon canola oil

1 teaspoon vanilla

### CARAMELIZED BANANAS

2 large bananas

Juice from 2 lemons

1 cup castor sugar

Juice from 1 orange

### CHOCOLATE SORBET

2 cups plus 2 tablespoons water

½ cup castor sugar (super-fine sugar)

½ cup glucose

7 ounces 70% dark chocolate, finely chopped (chef's choice is Valhrona)

½ teaspoon Staboline or invert sugar

### COCONUT SORBET

2 (13.5-ounce) cans coconut milk

1¾ cups plus 2 tablespoons sugar

1¾ cups plus 2 tablespoons water

1 lime, juiced

**To make the Bitter Chocolate Cake:** Preheat oven to 375 degrees F. Sift all dry ingredients together in a large bowl and mix well. In a separate bowl, combine the vinegar, water, oil, and vanilla. Add the liquid mixture to the dry ingredients and mix to form a smooth batter. Pour batter onto a parchment-lined 10 x 15-inch baking sheet, and bake in the center of the oven for 20 to 25 minutes, or until the top springs back when lightly pressed. Cool cake in the pan. Store in the refrigerator until ready to serve.

**To make the Carmelized Bananas:** Peel bananas and cut in half crosswise. Cut into 2-inch pieces to match the width of the chocolate cake pieces that are 2 x 4½ inches. Place bananas into a bowl with the juice of 1 lemon to prevent oxidization. Place sugar in a pan with enough water to allow it to dissolve. Add the remaining lemon juice and bring to a boil over high heat. Allow mixture to turn to a light caramel color and add the orange juice. Place bananas in the caramel and lower the heat. Cook until they begin to soften. Remove from the pan and place on a parchment-lined baking sheet; keep warm until ready to serve.

**To make the Chocolate Sorbet:** Boil the water with the sugar and glucose. Once it has reached a rolling boil, remove from heat and whisk in the chocolate. Add the inverted sugar and mix well. Pass mixture through a fine mesh strainer and cool completely at room temperature, making sure to whisk as it cools. Place mixture in an ice cream maker and process according to the manufacturer's directions.

**To make the Coconut Sorbet:** Pour coconut milk into a medium-size bowl. In a heavy saucepan, make a simple syrup by boiling the sugar and water together. As soon as it reaches a rolling boil, remove from the heat and pass through a fine mesh sieve. Pour the simple syrup

## CHOCOLATE SAUCE

3½ tablespoons cocoa powder

⅛ teaspoon salt

1 tablespoon cornstarch

1/2 cup castor sugar, divided

1 cup plus 2 teaspoons water

1.75 ounces 64% dark chocolate

## CHOCOLATE SPIKES

1 ounce cocoa liquor (i.e., 99% pure
   cocoa in block form)

½ cup granulated sugar

½ cup glucose or corn syrup

over the coconut milk. Add the lime juice and mix well; cool. Place cooled mixture into an ice cream maker and process according to the manufacturer's directions.

To make the Chocolate Sauce: Combine the cocoa powder, salt, cornstarch, and ¼ cup castor sugar in a medium bowl. In a saucepan, boil the water with the chocolate and remaining castor sugar. Pour boiled mixture into the cocoa powder mixture in the bowl. Mix well and return to the saucepan. Bring back to a boil and cook over a low heat for 5 minutes, continuously whisking. Pass through a fine mesh strainer and cool to room temperature.

To make the Chocolate Spikes: Chop the chocolate liquor. Cook the sugar and glucose or corn syrup to 165 degrees C or 329 degrees F. Add the chocolate to melt. Pour on top of parchment paper and roll out to a thickness that, although thin, will still be manageable to handle once cooled. Pre-cut into small squares; cool.

Separate the small squares and make into a powder in the food processor. Sift through a fine mesh sieve onto parchment paper and then melt in a 350-degree F oven. Using a small palette knife and powder-free latex gloves, pull the chocolate into desired long and fine pieces and cool, leaving one end strong enough to be inserted into the cake without breaking.

How to Plate: Cut the Bitter Chocolate Cake into 2 x 4½-inch pieces, making sure the width is the same as the width of the banana pieces. Generously brush the Chocolate Sauce across the plate, placing the cake in the center. Place the Caramelized Banana square on top of the cake at one end. Quenelle the Chocolate Sorbet and place near the center of the cake. At the desired place in the cake, make a slightly thin indent with a knife tip to help the end of the chocolate spikes to be placed and not break. Very gently anchor the tall Chocolate Spikes into the center. Make a larger quenelle of Coconut Sorbet and place on the end of the cake opposite the banana. Serve immediately.

# Todd English

*"If I were to be reincarnated as a vegetable, I would like to be a fava bean, hiding inside that little stem, living inside a velvet room!"*

Todd English began cooking at the age of fifteen and, in 1982, graduated from the Culinary Institute of America with honors. His culinary passion grew, working for Jacques Rachou at La Cote Basque in New York, and in Italy, he refined his interpretive rustic Mediterranean style. Returning to America at age twenty-five, he garnered acclaim as the chef at Michela's in Cambridge, Massachusetts, and in 1989, he opened Olives in Charlestown, Massachusetts. Today his restaurant brand stretches from New York and Connecticut to Aspen, Las Vegas, Seattle, and Washington, D.C. In 2006, Cunard's *Queen Mary 2,* Orlando's Blue Zoo at the Walt Disney World Resort's Dolphin Hotel, and Riche and 528 at Harrah's Hotel in New Orleans were added to the repertoire.

A noted chef and author of three acclaimed cookbooks, English has received three James Beard Foundation awards—Rising Star Chef (1991), Best Chef: Northeast (1994), and Who's Who in Food and Beverage in America. His other accolades include being a Nation's Restaurant News Top 50 Tastemaker, a *Bon Appétit* Restaurateur of the Year, and one of *People* magazine's (2001) 50 Most Beautiful People. In 2005, he served as executive celebrity chef for MTV's Video Music Awards; that same year, his collection of cookware and lifestyle products broke the housewares electronic retail record on HSN. His television credits include *Cooking Under Fire, Cooking with Todd English, Iron Chef USA, Good Morning America, Great Chefs of the Northeast,* and a thirteen-episode PBS international travel and cooking series—*Food Trip with Todd English.* His philanthropic endeavors include Big Brother, the Anthony Spinazzola Foundation, Share Our Strength, Boys and Girls Clubs, and City Year.

# *Crispy Artichoke alla Guidia with Eggless Caper Aioli*

## SERVES 4

### CRISPY ARTICHOKES

1 dozen baby artichokes

2 carrots, peeled and chopped

½ large Spanish onion, chopped

2 stalks celery, chopped

5 sprigs thyme

2 lemons

6 cloves garlic

1 cup white wine

1 quart water

3 tablespoons extra virgin olive
oil, divided

1 tablespoon salt, plus more
for seasoning

1 teaspoon black peppercorns

¼ cup flour

Pepper to taste

### AIOLI

3 slices white bread, crust removed

4 cloves garlic, crushed

1 teaspoon high-quality Dijon mustard

4 teaspoons sherry vinegar

1½ cups grapeseed oil

½ cup extra virgin olive oil

¼ cup salt-packed capers, washed
and drained

1 tablespoon finely chopped parsley

Juice of 1 lemon

Salt and pepper to taste

To make the Crispy Artichokes: Clean baby artichokes by soaking them in cold water. Pat dry, snap off the first layer or two of external leaves, and then cut off about one-third from the top. In a large covered pot, combine the artichokes, carrots, onion, celery, thyme, lemons, garlic, wine, water, 2 tablespoons oil, 1 tablespoon salt, and peppercorns, and cook artichokes until tender, about 20 minutes. Remove from liquid and place on a tray. Cool in refrigerator. Once cooled, slice in half. In a sauté pan, heat the remaining oil. Toss artichokes in flour and pan-fry, cut side down, until crispy and golden. Season with salt and pepper immediately; reserve.

If needed, before serving, reheat in oven at 375 degrees F for a few minutes until crisp.

NOTE: If using the "wagon wheels" as a garnish (see photo), fry them with the artichokes. They are store-bought preserved lemon slices, available in Middle Eastern resources.

To make the Aioli: On a cutting board, dice white bread and crush garlic. Place in a food processor and add mustard and vinegar. Begin to pulse, and slowly add grapeseed oil and then olive oil. Once emulsified, transfer to a bowl and add capers, parsley, and lemon juice. Season with salt and pepper. Cover and refrigerate.

## SALAD

1 teaspoon diced Calabrese peppers

Zest of 1 lemon, cut into strips, for salad and extra for garnish

¼ cup fresh Italian parsley leaves

¼ cup dry uncooked Moroccan couscous, cooked

6 thin red onion slices

## GARNISH

Lemon zest strips

Parsley

Wagon wheels

Caper berries, with stems

Small pieces of artichoke

Extra virgin olive oil

To make the Salad: In a bowl, combine peppers, zest, parsley, couscous, and onion. Toss in Crispy Artichokes.

How to Plate: Place a dollop of Aioli on the plate and top with the Salad. Add additional lemon zest strips and parsley on top. Place wagon wheels, caper berries, and artichoke pieces as desired. Drizzle with oil.

# Black Olive Pappardelle with Basil Pesto and Heirloom Tomato Salad

SERVES 4

## PAPPARDELLE

2 cups semolina flour

2 cups all-purpose flour

1 tablespoon high-quality black
   olive purée

½ to 1 cup water

## BASIL PESTO

1 bunch fresh basil, picked and
   cleaned

1 cup spinach, picked and cleaned

½ cup pine nuts, toasted

4 cloves garlic

1 teaspoon crushed red pepper

1½ cups extra virgin olive oil

Salt and pepper to taste

## HEIRLOOM SALAD

4 to 6 medium-size heirloom tomatoes
   (red, black, and green)

½ tablespoon extra virgin olive oil

Salt to taste

## TOASTED GARLIC BREADCRUMBS

1 small loaf day-old rustic bread,
   crust removed

1 tablespoon extra virgin olive oil

6 cloves garlic, diced

1 teaspoon diced parsley

To make the Pappardelle: Place flours in a bowl and mix well. Make a well at the bottom and stir in black olive purée and water; mix until well incorporated. Once dough is formed, make a ball and let it rest for 15 minutes. Roll out dough on a pasta machine until desired thickness—the number 1 setting on a standard pasta machine is best. With a chef's knife or pizza cutter, cut 1½-inch strips of pappardelle. Refrigerate until ready to cook.

To cook, add pasta to salted boiling water and cook for 2 minutes, or to desired doneness.

NOTE: Store-bought egg-free noodle pasta can be substituted.

To make the Basil Pesto: Place all ingredients in a food processor and pulse until desired consistency. Adjust seasoning with salt and pepper.

To make the Heirloom Salad: Cut some tomatoes into quarters and some into slices. Season with oil and salt; reserve until plating.

To make the Toasted Garlic Breadcrumbs: Cut the bread into small cubes. In a bowl, toss the bread with oil and garlic until well coated. Transfer bread to a pan and cook over medium heat, tossing until all sides of the cubes are evenly toasted. Place crunchy cubes in a food processor and pulse into crumbs. Toss in parsley and pulse.

## ELEPHANT GARLIC CHIPS AND FRIED BASIL LEAVES

2 cups oil for frying (canola is option)

4 elephant garlic cloves, or more, sliced

1 bunch fresh basil, washed, dried, and leaves removed

Salt to taste

## GARNISH

Black olives, pitted and cut into quarters, 3 to 4 whole olives per serving

To make the Elephant Garlic Chips and Fried Basil Leaves: Heat oil until almost smoking point, at least 350 degrees F. Carefully avoid splatters while adding garlic until golden brown, less than a minute. Remove with slotted spoon and drain on paper towels. Salt to taste. In same oil, drop handfuls of basil leaves into the oil to crisp in seconds. With a slotted spoon lift onto paper towels and serve while crisp.

How to Plate: Create a wide strip of Basil Pesto on one side of the plate. Place Pappardelle in a strip alongside the pesto and sprinkle with olives and Elephant Garlic Chips. Position Heirloom Salad in a strip alongside the pasta. Sprinkle with Toasted Garlic Breadcrumbs and top with a few Fried Basil Leaves.

# Pastrami Tofu with Pumpernickel Farro and Whole Grain Mustard

SERVES 4

## PASTRAMI TOFU

⅔ cup crushed juniper

½ cup black peppercorns, crushed

4 cups water

1 cup light brown sugar

1 cup salt

3 tablespoons black pepper

6 teaspoons dried thyme

9 bay leaves

3 tablespoons coriander

2 teaspoons ground cloves

To make the Pastrami Tofu: Combine the juniper and crushed peppercorns, set aside. Add all remaining ingredients except tofu into a saucepot and bring to a boil. Remove from heat and chill liquid. Submerge tofu in brine for 2 hours. Remove, pat dry and coat with the juniper and peppercorn mixture. Place on a tray and broil for 3 to 4 minutes, or until golden brown.

12 cloves garlic

6 teaspoons juniper

4 (6-ounce) blocks extra-firm tofu

## FARRO

1 cup farro

2 cups water

2 tablespoons cocoa powder

2 shots espresso

3 teaspoons caraway, toasted and
then ground, divided

2 teaspoons blended oil (90%
vegetable oil/10% olive oil)

## FRIED PICKLE CHIPS

2 whole sour pickles, sliced in
half lengthwise

1 tablespoon all-purpose flour

1 teaspoon cayenne pepper

Oil for frying

## WHOLE GRAIN
## MUSTARD VINAIGRETTE

1 tablespoon whole grain mustard

4 teaspoons water

1 teaspoon red wine vinegar

1 teaspoon soy sauce

## BEET JUICE

6 medium-size beets

## GARNISH

2 dill pickles for plating, cut
in half lengthwise

8 sprigs chives, cut into
2-inch pieces

To make the Farro: In a saucepan, combine farro, water, cocoa powder, espresso, and 1 teaspoon caraway. Cook for 20 minutes, or until tender, and then strain and cool. In a hot sauté pan, add oil and fry the farro mixture until crispy. Season with remaining caraway.

To make the Fried Pickle Chips: Dredge pickles in flour and pepper. Deep-fry in oil for 4 minutes at 350 degrees F, or until crispy; reserve.

To make the Whole Grain Mustard Vinaigrette: In a small bowl, whisk ingredients together. Combine with the Farro.

To make the Beet Juice: Peel and juice beets using a vegetable juicer. In a saucepan, reduce liquid until it is a syrupy consistency; reserve.

How to Plate: Using a spoon or brush, paint a thick line of Beet Juice across two sides of the plate, making an L-shape. Slice Pastrami Tofu into 4 thick slices and arrange on the Beet Juice, sprinkling with any extra juniper and peppercorn mixture. Place half dill pickle on an angle to one corner of the plate. Place a dollop of the Whole Grain Mustard Vinaigrette and Farro mixture on top of the pickle. Add Fried Pickle Chips to garnish. Sprinkle plate with chive pieces and remaining caraway seeds.

# Soy Milk Panna Cotta with Crushed Blackberries and Vanilla Muscat Sauce

## PANNA COTTA

4 cups soy milk

⅓ cup white beet sugar

1 vanilla bean, scraped for seeds

3½ teaspoons agar-agar powder

## BLACKBERRY SAUCE

1 pint fresh blackberries

2 tablespoons white beet sugar

Pinch of salt

## VANILLA MUSCAT SAUCE

2 cups Muscat de Beaumes
   sweet wine

¼ cup apricot jam

½ vanilla bean, scraped

## GARNISH

Finely ground pepper

Fresh red raspberries, blueberries,
   blackberries, red seedless grapes

Micro greens

To make the Panna Cotta: Combine soy milk, sugar, and vanilla bean and seeds. Bring to a simmer, add the agar-agar powder and stir well. Bring to a boil and cook for 2 minutes. Remove the vanilla bean, and then pour the milk into 2-ounce ramekins; chill for 1 hour.

To make the Blackberry Sauce: Place the blackberries, sugar, and salt in a bowl. Gently crush the blackberries with a fork until they start releasing their juices. Marinate for 10 minutes. In a small sauté pan over medium-high heat, cook berries for 5 minutes, or until juices start to thicken; cool.

To make the Vanilla Muscat Sauce: Place all the ingredients into a small saucepan, including the vanilla bean, and bring to a boil. Remove the vanilla bean and allow sauce to cool to room temperature.

How to Plate: Dip one of the Panna Cotta ramekins in warm water for 5 seconds and then invert into a small bowl. Spoon Vanilla Muscat Sauce around the Panna Cotta. Sprinkle lightly with ground pepper, and then top with Blackberry Sauce along one side. Garnish with fresh berries, grapes, and micro greens.

# Glossary

AGAR-AGAR: The vegetarian equivalent to animal-derived gelatin. Agar-agar, used as a thickener or stabilizer, is a transparent substance, available in flakes, powder, or strands. It is derived from several species of red sea weed.

AGAVE NECTAR (OR SYRUP): Natural liquid sweetener made from the extract of the wild agave, a succulent plant mainly grown in Mexico. It is sweeter and more mild tasting than honey, and has a low glycemic index making it useful for diabetics. A good substitute for sugar and other sweeteners.

BATTONET: A French cutting term in which the food item is cut into 2½ x ¼ x ¼-inch-long narrow strips. The length requested can vary up to 4 inches.

BLANCH: To plunge a small amount of a vegetable or herb into boiling water or oil, usually seconds to a minute, maintaining a constant boiling temperature. It is done to set color, remove skins and or lightly soften. The ingredient is then plunged into an ice water bath (shocked) to stop the cooking process.

BLOOMED: Soaking an ingredient, often dried fruits, to create a softened texture that results in a whitish surface.

BRAISE: A cooking method by which food is first browned in fat, then cooked tightly covered in a small amount of liquid at low heat for a lengthy period of time to develop flavor and tenderize food by gently breaking down their fibers.

BRUNOISE: A French cutting term in which the food item is first julienned and then turned 90 degrees and diced again producing cubes. It must be very consistent in size and shape.

CARRAGEENAN: Made from Irish Moss, a dried red algae, used as a thickening, stabilizing, emulsifying or suspending agent. When softened in water, it will form a jelly.

CASTOR SUGAR: Super-fine sugar seen in British recipes. Dissolves faster in foods and can be made by grinding regular sugar if unable to find.

CHAAT MASALA: Hugely popular tangy hot-sour Indian spice mix, typically consisting of green mango powder, cumin, black salt, coriander, dried ginger, salt, black pepper, asafetida, and red pepper.

COCONUT MEAT: The flesh from the inside of a young coconut. The "meat" is soft and gelatinous and contains very nutritious coconut water. They are sold wrapped in clear plastic and reveal their white color and slightly pointed top.

CONFIT: A French term for food immersed in salt, sugar, or vinegar, and some slow roasted in the oven with an oil coating. It is one of the oldest ways to preserve food.

DEGLAZE: To dissolve cooking juices and dark clinging particles in which food has been sautéed or roasted by adding liquid and stirring.

DICE: A small cubed dice is a ¼ x ¼ x ¼-inch square. A medium dice is a ½ x ½ x ½-inch square and a large dice is a ¾ x ¾ x ¾-inch square.

FARRO: An original grain from which all others are derived. Ground into a paste and cooked, it is the primary ingredient in polenta.

GLUCOSE: A simple sugar that browns at a lower temperature than other sugars and is highly effective in preventing crystallization. Useful in sugar mixtures for pulling and shaping without cracking and breaking.

GOJI BERRIES: Grown on an evergreen shrub in the China region, usually dried and look like red raisins. They are rich in antioxidants.

GRAINS OF PARADISE: A large-grained spice native to the west coast of Africa with a zesty flavor reminiscent of pepper, coriander and cardamom.

GREEN MANGOES: The native green mango is similar in flavor and texture to a crisp, tart, green apple.

HAKUREI TURNIPS: A young Japanese turnip that has flat, round, smooth, and white roots and a sweet and fruity flavor.

HIJIKI: Seaweed that comes in short matchstick-sized black strips and best used in dishes requiring simmering.

ISOMALT: The only sugar replica made from pure sugar but tastes as naturally sweet as sugar. An inverted sugar that is easier to work and resists humidity.

JULIENNE: To cut food into ½ x ⅛ x 3-inch length strips.

MEYER LEMON: A hybrid between a lemon and an orange or a mandarin. Less acidic than a lemon.

MICRO GREENS: Known as the smallest edible plants on Earth. They are really just sprouts grown in a moisture-retaining medium, which grow vertically. Almost any tiny seed can be grown this way, and are harvested after they form their first true leaves.

MIRIN RICE WINE: A very sweet Japanese wine used to flavor rice and sauces, and is not for drinking. A substitute is 1 tablespoon dry sherry plus ½ teaspoon sugar or white wine and sugar to taste.

NAMA SHOYU: A raw unpasteurized soy sauce with a rich, full-bodied flavor, plus healthful living enzymes.

OPAL BASIL: A variety of basil also known as purple-leaf basil. It has dark, purple-red leaves, stems, and flowers.

PEDRO XIMENEZ (PX): Spanish sweet dessert wine some consider as one of the best in the world. Used in the production of sherry for sweetening and comes from a white grape of the same name.

QUENELLE: The decorative shape of a neat, three-sided oval formed by smoothing a spoonful of mixture between the bowls of two rotating spoons. Often used in the plating presentations of sorbets, ice creams, and soft topping and mimics the shape of an egg.

SALSIFY (GOATS BEARD): A white fleshy root shaped like a parsnip with slight oyster or artichoke heart taste.

SEAR: To quickly brown the surface of food by exposing it to extremely high heat.

SILPAT: A popular brand name for a flexible nonstick food-grade silicone baking mat. Delicate cooking procedures are made possible by using it.

SIMPLE SYRUP: A 2 to 1 ratio mixture of sugar and water. Made by using two parts sugar to one part water and dissolving in boiling water. Some recipes prefer 2 to 2 or other ratios.

SUCANAT: A brand name for a popular unrefined sugar made from pure dried sugar cane juice. It retains its molasses content and can be used as a substitute for brown sugar.

SUJI: An Indian reference for a wheat semolina grain.

SUNCHOKE (JERUSALEM ARTICHOKES): A root of a plant in the sunflower family that looks like bulbous gingerroots with many stubby outcroppings. The ivory flesh is similar to water chestnuts and tastes of artichokes and salsify.

SWEAT: To cook vegetables quickly over high heat usually with a little oil until crisp-tender.

TAMARIND: An Indian date, a key ingredient in Indian cooking. The pods contain seeds and sour-sweet pulp that, when dried, become very sour.

TOFU (REGULAR): Chinese-style tofu, it is made by coagulating soy milk, and then pressing the resulting curds into blocks. It is best used in stir-frys or any dish where you want to retain its shape.

TOFU (SILKEN): Japanese-style tofu, it has a softer consistency than regular tofu and falls apart easily. It is often sold in an aseptic package and is best used in salad dressings, sauces, and desserts where a creamy texture is desired.

TOKYO TURNIPS: About the size of a red radish but with a white skin and interior. It has a mild flavor and is usually eaten raw.

TRUFFLES (TUBER): A hard, rough, irregular round mushroom found near tree roots and grown underground. A highly-prized and expensive food, that is the size of a walnut up to an apple, with a delicate earthy smell and served raw in paper-thin slices as a topping. Black (France) and White (Italy and U.S.) truffles are found by trained dogs and female pigs, between September and May.

TRUFFLES (CHOCOLATE): A confection made with a ganache center (mixture of chocolate and dairy, or dairy substitutes, in 2 to1 ratio) coated with chocolate or cocoa powder, usually in bite-sized balls. Other fillings and coatings can be used.

TRUFFLE OIL: It is created by soaking truffles in olive oil. The aroma of truffle oil is earthy and only a few drops are needed for flavoring.

UMEBOSHI PLUM PASTE: A zesty purée made from the flesh of salt pickled umeboshi plums. Adds tartness and saltiness to salads, spreads, sauces, and vegetables.

VIDALIA ONIONS: An unusually sweet onion grown in a production area defined by law in Georgia. They are available from April to mid-June.

WHEAT BERRIES: Whole unprocessed wheat kernels, the whole grain containing the endosperm, bran, and germ, thus all fiber and nutrients are still intact.

# Index

### Metric Conversion Chart

Liquid and Dry Measures

| U.S. | Canadian | Australian |
|------|----------|------------|
| ¼ teaspoon | 1 mL | 1 ml |
| ½ teaspoon | 2 mL | 2 ml |
| 1 teaspoon | 5 mL | 5 ml |
| 1 tablespoon | 15 mL | 20 ml |
| ¼ cup | 50 mL | 60 ml |
| ⅓ cup | 75 mL | 80 ml |
| ½ cup | 125 mL | 125 ml |
| ⅔ cup | 150 mL | 170 ml |
| ¾ cup | 175 mL | 190 ml |
| 1 cup | 250 mL | 250 ml |
| 1 quart | 1 liter | 1 litre |

### Temperature Conversion Chart

| Fahrenheit | Celsius |
|------------|---------|
| 250 | 120 |
| 275 | 140 |
| 300 | 150 |
| 325 | 160 |
| 350 | 180 |
| 375 | 190 |
| 400 | 200 |
| 425 | 220 |
| 450 | 230 |
| 475 | 240 |
| 500 | 260 |

Alex Stratta

Anne Quatrano

David Burke

Bradford Thompson

Floyd Cardoz

Cat Cora

Suzanne Goin

Daniel Boulud

Jean-Georges Vongerichten

Marcus Samuelsson

Josef Huber

Michel Nischan